The Tale of
TWO
BEARS

DENVER, COLORADO

This book is dedicated to my father,

Marvin Rutledge
(Jan. 1942-Aug. 2015)

Who has always been there for me
and molded me into the man I am today.

Contents

Introduction..i

Part One: The Early Years 1
Chapter 1: My Tribe...3
Chapter 2: Grandpa..8
Chapter 3: Grandma...20
Chapter 4: Growing Wild 25
Chapter 5: Edumacating 31
Chapter 6: Street Rods and Motorcycles 39

Part Two: Somewhere in Between 45
Chapter 1: Hunting and Shenanigans.....................47
Chapter 2: Birds of a Feather...................................57
Chapter 3: Adventures Above and Below Sea Level 66

Part Three: The Badge...81
Chapter 1: Introduction 83
Chapter 2:The Secret, Secret Task Force 91

Part Four: In Pursuit of the Dream 99
Chapter 1: Within Sight 101
Chapter 2: Dream Part Deux............................114
Chapter 3: The Wolves....................................119
Chapter 4: Settling In 126

Epilogue: The Wife's Perspective 139
Photo Album 147

Introduction

MY JOURNEY - from humble beginnings running wild through the shinnery in Hawley, Texas – to my life as a secret task force agent in the war on drugs – to living my dream as a mountain man and opening Two Bears Trading Post - is a jagged one. And like any man, I wear my scars like a badge of honor. It has always been my experience that any road worth traveling usually comes with dust billowing, gravel flying and a rut or two to keep you humble.

These are the stories of the road I travelled, the kinfolk I call my people and some of the friends I've met along the way. It isn't always pretty, and it damn sure isn't politically correct, but if in the end it inspires you to follow your dreams, think a little deeper or even brings a smile to your face, it's served its purpose. This is the tale of Two Bears.

Part One
The Early Years

CHAPTER 1

My Tribe

I WAS BORN in the month of the popping leaves, when the Aspens shiver in the October wind, their golden quivers dancing in the changing light. I took my first breath on a day dedicated to remembering the dead. It was All Hallow's Eve, 1963, and I was the second child born to Marvin and Heidi Rutledge.

My dad was three-quarters Cherokee and one-quarter German. He was a soldier in the U.S. Army stationed in Frankfurt, Germany. Tensions were high as the Vietnam War was just getting into full swing. During his deployment he met my mom, a German citizen. Dad knew enough German to ask her out for a date, and well, things progressed along nicely. They married, and started a family. Their first child, my sister Donna, was born in Germany, and after returning to the U.S. in 1963, they welcomed me into the world at the Ft. Lewis Army Base in Tacoma, Washington.

My mother's father was also a soldier. He and his twin brother fought side by side under Hitler's regime during WWII. My

Opa was perforated with seven bullet holes across his chest, arms, and legs and was sewn up by German field medics who pumped him full of methamphetamine. He and his wounded brother were seeking safety in the trenches when a German Sargent came up behind them, held a gun to their heads and threatened to kill them if they didn't return to the field.

My Opa heeded the warning and continued to fight until he passed out from the loss of blood, but not before watching his twin brother get shot in the head. Opa was found, barely alive, by the American Red Cross who gave him blood and the medical care he needed, saving his life. During one of his many trips to the U.S. to visit us, I remember, as a young boy, staring at his many scars from those wounds. If it hadn't been for the American Red Cross, I wouldn't exist.

We didn't live in Washington for very long. Dad completed his service for the U.S. and moved us to his mother's house in the small town of Hawley, Texas. Most of the people who resided in Hawley were my relatives – aunts, uncles, and many, many cousins. There were no jobs to be had at that time in Hawley, so dad sought and eventually found work in a manufacturing facility in Dallas, Texas.

My mom had a difficult time transitioning into her new life in a new country. The relationship between this stern German woman and my Cherokee father was many times volatile, creating an environment wrought with tension. During those years I escaped the turmoil by staying outside; it's where I've always felt most comfortable. Because of that mom shaved my head as she could rarely get me inside to bathe. She said I was nothing but a grubby, dirty little boy.

Mom and dad stuck it out together for several years but eventually their tumultuous marriage ended in divorce. My sister Donna and I chose to stay with my father.

It was during that time that my dad found work as a police officer in Abilene. He wasn't much for being without a woman, and with two young'un's to tend to, he quickly found himself another wife. I think he knew right away he'd made a mistake when he married Pam. The woman nearly cost me my life. She chased me through a wheat field in her Volkswagen Bug one day after school because I'd come home hungry and was fixing to eat "her" grapes. She stormed out of the room, returning with a thick rawhide belt. It didn't take a rocket scientist to know what she intended to do with it, and when I saw her fat ass coming at me with it, I bolted out the back door, running as fast as I could into a neighboring wheat field. I could hear the whine of the engine, tires crashing and crunching through the field behind me as I ran. She tried her damnedest to run me over.

Fortunately, my sister saw what was going on and called my dad telling him he needed to get home ASAP. "Pam's trying to kill Mark," she screamed hysterically into the phone. I managed to avert getting run over by that crazy woman, but the wheat field took its toll on my young body. I was a cut up, bloody mess by the time my dad came screeching into the driveway. That was the last we saw of Pam, and believe me when I tell you there was no one happier than me to see her go.

Dad must've had them waiting in line because without skipping a beat, Linda appeared. Linda was looking for work, my dad owned a gas station and he gave her a job. She moved in a month later and eventually they were married. She must have been the glue that stuck. She was at my father's bedside when he passed away. They were married 38 years.

CHAPTER 2

Grandpa

MY GRANDMA AND Grandpa were something else. Despite all of the turmoil at home, they enriched my life and brought laughter and meaning to it beyond measure. Many life lessons were learned sitting at their kitchen table. There were also a handful of others who directly impacted my life and helped shape who and what I am today. My story would not be complete without them.

It was my grandpa who awakened me to the feel of adrenaline coursing through my veins and the rush that came with it. It would become a high that, to this day, I cannot live without. And it was through his nightly storytelling, that I learned the value of a tale well-told, always resulting in a generous heaping of the best medicine - laughter.

My grandpa's name was JC Rutledge and he was a character. He was Choctaw, Chickasha, Cherokee and German, but he looked like a full-blooded German. He was raised down in the valley of Texas and he had one brother and one sister.

My grandpa left home when he was 14 years old., his 12-year-old brother at his side. Times were hard at home and food was scarce, and the two boys set out penniless and alone on foot looking for work. They headed north because word was work was more plentiful there. He and his brother slept under overpasses and bridges at night, and when I was a kid we'd sit around the kitchen table and he'd tell me stories about those days while he smoked his filterless Camel cigarettes and sipped his vodka … wearing nothing but his boxer shorts.

When he and his brother left home, my grandpa's only possessions were the clothes on his back and an old guitar – and, boy, could he sing. He and his brother walked hundreds of miles, hitching rides when they could, always stopping off in the dusty towns along the way. He'd sling open the guitar case on city sidewalks and the two boys would sing for the town folk, hoping to collect enough change so they could eat.

On his way north, his route took him through Hawley, Texas just outside of Abilene. That's where my grandma lived. Grandma was Cherokee. She was 15 years old at the time, the oldest of nine kids, and she worked out in the cotton fields.

My grandpa and his brother saw her working in the field as they were making their way down an old dirt road one day and she caught my grandpa's eye. As luck – or fate - would have it, my grandma's daddy saw the hungry boys and offered them lunch. Not wanting to miss an opportunity to get closer to the little Indian girl that had caught his fancy, he asked her father if he had need for a couple of extra hands in the field. And again, as luck would have it, he did. Grandpa told me the only reason he wanted to pick cotton was so he could spend some time with my grandmother. He was smitten.

News reached Grandpa that there were jobs to be had in the oilfields of Midland, Texas, 500 miles west. He began making his way by walking and hitching rides with generous travelers, determined to get to Midland. Out of desperation he stole a 1934 Model A from a man's front yard and used it to reach his destination. He made enough money to buy a 1929 Model A for his return to Hawley to see my grandmother. He bought the car for $5 and fixed it up so at the end of his work week, he could get back home. That scrap heap, he said, was left on the side of the highway when the transmission shelled after one trip. All the same, his persistence paid off.

He and my grandma married and had three kids: James, Joyce and Marvin, my dad. Joyce , who had polio as a child, married a man named Dan Baldwin. They moved in with my grandparents where they all lived together. Joyce had one son, my cousin Danny, and the two of us would become inseparable. James married Diane, and they had two children. Diane would become one of those special people who had a direct impact on the man that I am today.

White Lightning

We're all a little off in my family. We've got bikers, vets, cowboys, and Indians. You would be wise not to mess with my family lest you were looking to get hurt. From an outsider's point of view, my family was straight out of the movie Deliverance. (You talk about hearing banjos play.) We lived on a wild and wooly chunk of land called the shinnery and you just didn't mess with the folks who lived there; especially if they were part of the Jordan clan, which was pretty much everyone.

My Grandpa was known in the area as Big Jake, he was 6'3 and weighed 250 pounds. He spent two years in jail for running moonshine in '56. During that time there were no jobs to be had, so my Grandpa distilled white lightening and sold it to a guy in Stamford, Texas. Well, when I was a little boy, my cousin Danny and I got to go on one of those moonshine runs with Grandpa. It was around the summer of '68 and Danny and I weren't but 5 years old. We had no TV, no radio, no electricity and no running water. We took our baths in number two washtubs and lived on dirt floors. There wasn't much for a kid to do but hang out by the river, fish, hunt and listen to the men pick guitars and banjos on the front porch after dinner. So, for Danny and I, a run with Grandpa was an adventure too good to pass up.

Grandpa had a 1951 Plymouth with a 426 hemi Chrysler engine in it with cut outs on the exhaust. It had a bench seat in the front. He had a cut out in the trunk with 2 x 12s crossed over each other. Each slot was filled with hay where he nestled the Mason jars full of his white lightning and then covered them with a blanket.

There was an old gravel road in front of the house and it was the back road to Stamford.

Danny and I jumped in the car and down the road we went, Big Jake at the wheel. Danny and I were jumping up and down with excitement in the backseat and I remember Grandpa was jolly that day. We were off and running on a big, new adventure.

Back then, the old black and white cop cars had a single cherry on the top. Before long Grandpa heard the sirens, and so did I. I was standing on the back seat looking out the window and yelled, "Grandpa! The cops are behind us!" Grandpa glanced in the rearview mirror and shouted, "You boys sit down and hang on."

Grandpa reached down and pulled a lever on the side of his seat. At the time I didn't know what it was, but I remember the car got really, really loud. It was the cut outs - a rod he'd put in there that opened the exhaust so it would run better. It would blow the exhaust straight down into the dirt and not only did the car take off like a bat out of hell, it stirred the dirt up, too, leaving anyone behind you in a cloud of dust.

We were on our knees looking out the back window when Grandpa floored the gas pedal. I never will forget that cloud of dust billowing up like a bomb had detonated behind us, and off we went, flying down the road like a roller coaster ride. That cop didn't stand a chance.

We made it to Stamford and Grandpa parked the car in front of an old rundown shack. The first thing I saw when the door opened was a sawed off double barrel shotgun, followed by the biggest, blackest-haired white man I'd ever seen. He scared me to death. The man looked exactly like I imagined the devil would look.

The men finished their business, and Grandpa said, "Boys, let's go to the drug store." Hell, we didn't even know what the drug store was but if Grandpa wanted to go there, we figured we were in for more excitement. Well, Grandpa took us to the drug store in Anson, Texas and it was the first time I ever had a real coke. Back then it was an old fashioned soda fountain and you could make a coke that would wind your ass up. I never will forget how good that was.

The cops never did find us, and Danny and I had a ball. It was fun as hell. From that moment on, if Grandpa was doing a run, we wanted to go. We had officially become adrenaline junkies and had discovered our own brand of white lightning – Coca Cola.

Hit the Gas

Running the roads with Big Jake was always an adventure, even before you got out of the driveway. I remember another time Grandpa was making a run to *get* liquor. You see, back then Abilene was dry and Hawley was just outside of Abilene. You couldn't get whiskey or liquor so you had to go to Pinkies liquor store. Pinkies was located on the outskirts of Abilene, in the city of Impact. The liquor store was the only reason the town of Impact even existed.

Grandpa had already drank a little bit before we had gotten in the car, and Danny was jumping around in the front seat a whooping and hollering. Now Grandpa had diabetes and his size 14 feet swelled up real bad so he always wore a pair of huge basketball shoes. To this day I don't know why he did this, but he'd pump the hell out of that accelerator to get that old Ford ready to start. Then he'd give it too much gas backing out of the driveway because he couldn't feel his feet, and whether there was a car coming or not, we'd yell "Grandpa, there's a car coming!" and he'd slam on the brakes and we'd go sailing over the back seat. We'd roll around in the backseat laughing and giggling. And every time he'd look back at us and say, "Damned people don't know how to drive."

Damn Kids

Like I said, we were poor and there wasn't much to do in the shinnery but fish, hunt or trap, and sometimes messing with Grandpa was our preferred form of entertainment.

It was July 4th weekend and I was about 14 years old. My cousin Danny and I had been to the fireworks stand and bought some of those little sticks that explode, you know, with the little plastic explosives on them? Well, Danny kept Grandpa distracted while I got his pack of cigarettes. I stuck a little explosive inside two or three of his Camels and pushed them back in the pack where he could smoke two or three cigarettes without realizing the pack had been tampered with.

So there we were, sitting around the table eating supper, laughing, and telling jokes, and listening to Grandpa while he's drinking his vodka and getting drunk again. My Grandma was right across from Grandpa, and Danny and I were at the table when Grandpa lit up his fourth Camel cigarette. He had it in his mouth, took a deep drag off of his cigarette and ka-boom, the firecracker caught the spark and blew that cigarette all to hell, out of his mouth, blowing ashes and shit and tobacco all over my Grandma. My Grandpa, who just about shit his britches, yelled, "Son of a bitch!" And Grandma yelled, "What the hell?" Startled by the blast we all jumped up knocking everything off the table. Grandma would have beat us to death but Danny and I were out the door before she could catch us, tears rolling downs our cheeks from laughing so hard. We could hear Grandpa in the kitchen yelling "You little son of a bitch!" It was funny The look on his face with part of the cigarette still stuck in his mouth, all curled up on the end was funny and still makes me laugh to this day. Looking back, I guess we could have blown the poor fella's lips off.

From that day forward Grandpa always took a closer look at his Camels before he put one to his mouth and lit the flame … and he kept a wary eye on us.

Welcome to the Family

Dad, now twice divorced, had just started dating his soon to be third wife, Linda, and decided it was time to introduce her to the family.

Grandpa used to sit around the kitchen table in his underwear because it was always hotter than hell. The only form of air conditioning they had was from an old swamp cooler and the cool air never seemed to get to the back of the house. He'd sit there at the table and smoke his cigarettes,, hell, he'd smoke so many that his fingers turned yellow from the tar. Every night he was perched there at the table, smoking and drinking - he'd drink almost a pint of vodka every night. He was funny. He'd tell jokes and we'd laugh, my cousin Danny and I.

On the chosen night, dad took Linda over to meet my grandparents unannounced, and, as usual, Grandpa was sitting at the kitchen table, drinking, in his underwear. Now, Linda always dressed real nice, you know, real feminine like. She didn't really belong with us country folk. She and my dad just popped in, and my dad says, "Hey, mom and dad. I just wanted to introduce Linda to you."

Dad and Linda took a seat at the table. My Grandpa, in his underwear and seeing this pretty gal dressed in all her finery, said," Well, I wish you'd have told me sooner so I could have put on some clothes." Dad assured him it was alright, Grandpa, drunk and embarrassed, got up, waddling and tripping over himself with Linda sitting right there, her hands covering her face trying to hide a look that said, "Oh my Gosh, what am I doing here." Well, in all that waddling and tripping

Grandpa's shorts fell off. Those loose boxer shorts, they fell right smack down around his ankles, and when they did he said "Oh my goodness!" And Linda looked and said "Oh, my God!" and when Grandpa was bent over with his white-ass cheeks in her face trying to retrieve his boxers, he farted.

We all lost it - even Grandma –and she didn't laugh a whole lot. Linda turned and she gave us the funniest look I've ever seen in my life.

Turned out there was a pretty tough gal underneath all those pretty clothes. She soon fell right in with all of us wild heathens, and loved us just the same. She loved Dad even more, she married him, and God bless her, stayed by his side till the end.

Parting Words

In his later years, Grandpa worked at the state school driving buses and playing Santa Claus for all the people there. For all his faults, I loved that man. My Grandpa had diabetes and didn't take care of himself. On his deathbed he told me that all he'd ever really wanted to be was a captain on a fishing boat in the Gulf. The last time I saw him he was quiet for a moment and said, "Mark, don't be like me. Go chase your dreams." Those words have propelled me through doubt and discouragement many times since I pulled up anchor and set sail for my dreams. Grandpa's dream never got off the shore but he set the compass and pointed me toward the open water. I like to think it's because that's exactly what real captains do.

CHAPTER 3

Grandma

MY GRANDMOTHER, ALFA Mae Jordan, was full-blooded Cherokee and we had a special bond. She was beautiful, with the softest skin and the silkiest, long black hair I'd ever seen. She had the truest heart of anyone I knew. She was my anchor, my protector and the balm that eased my conflicted spirit. She carried within her the gift of visions, something I would come to have an intimate understanding of as I grew older. It is because of my grandmother and her ability to see what others could not that I am known as Two Bears.

"You don't eat where you pee"

While dad was building us a house, we were living with Grandma in her two-room shack in Hawley where you could literally see through the walls. In the winter we'd get the cotton balls that were left in the bottom of our cotton sacks and stuff them in the cracks of the walls to keep out the draft. We had no running water and no electricity. If you wanted water you'd have to head outside with your bucket and a rope and lower it down into a hand-dug cistern, and if you had to go to the restroom you'd have to go to the outhouse, or just pee outside off the porch.

Eventually, we moved Grandma into a house with plumbing and electricity in the big city of Abilene. It was the first time she had ever been exposed to indoor plumbing. She wasn't familiar with it at all, and was baffled by the fact that you could turn on the faucet and have water come in. I guess it was in the early '70s. I was just a kid and I remember the day Dad delivered her to her new home. He was giving her the nickel tour and showing her where the bathroom was. Grandma stood there in amazement for a few minutes taking it all in, then turned to my Dad and matter-of-factly stated, "I'll be damned if I'm gonna pee in the house where I eat."

At that time Dad was an officer for the Abilene Police Department and during this time Abilene was a very small town where everyone knew everyone. I remember Dad telling me, "I was on patrol today, and I got a call about a lady who was seen peeing outside in the backyard. I'll be damned if it wasn't my own mom!"

The dispatcher had called him over the radio and said, "Marvin, you need to go talk to your mom. She's outside using the restroom in her back yard." So, bewildered, Dad went to her and asked, "Mom, why are you doing this?" And once again, that tough old gal answered, "I told you, I ain't gonna pee in the house that I eat in!"

It took a while and a lot of sweet talking, but my Dad finally convinced her to use the restroom in the house, and eventually she became comfortable with it. The poor gal had never used anything but an outhouse her entire life.

To add insult to injury, about a year later my cousin Danny and I were sitting on the living room floor at Grandma's playing with our Hot Wheels when we heard her screaming in the bathroom. She was sitting on the toilet and a big sewer rat had come up out of the toilet, crawled out from between her legs and started running around in the bathroom. Grandma was screaming and cussing like a sailor. When we finally got the door open, there she was, standing there throwing whatever she could get her hands on at that rat. We watched as it jumped back on the seat, dove into the toilet and headed back down into the sewer system. Evidently, the rat had been doing it for a while, coming up out of the toilet long enough to eat food before heading back down into the murky underworld of human waste.

Grandma's rear end never made contact with a toilet seat again. From that day forward she hovered over the toilet. The rat had only strengthened her resolve that "eating where you pee" was a bad idea no matter how convenient indoor plumbing might be........

The Hardest Goodbye

My Grandma spent her whole life waiting hand and foot on Grandpa. Outside of working the cotton fields as a young girl, she never held a job. Her sole purpose in life was to take care of my Grandfather.

After Grandpa died, I 'm certain Grandma felt lost, with nothing left to live for. She lasted just a year after Grandpa, and I'm convinced she died of a broken heart.

I was 18 at the time she passed and I was in the process of building my own house in Hawley. It took a while but I finally talked her into coming out there to see it even though it wasn't completed yet. It wasn't long after that she passed away.

When she was on her deathbed, it was just the two of us alone. Knowing how close we were, Dad had graciously left the room to give me some time alone with her. She looked at me through her fading eyes and whispered, "I'm sorry," and then took her last breath, shattering my heart into a million pieces.

After she passed away of course everything changed. We'd always had Thanksgiving and Christmas dinner over at her house. The whole family was always there. She was the nucleus that brought everyone together. When she died the family kind of splintered, and like many families, everyone went their separate ways.

She didn't talk about it, but everyone knew. Like many Native Americans, Grandma possessed a unique gift from the time she was a child. She saw visions, and I believe it was through a vision that she gave me the name Two Bears. She said that there were two bears that lived within me, always in conflict, fighting for dominance. Grandma knew there was something different about me but we never discussed it. I think she was aware that I could see things. I had always thought the way I saw things was normal, just assumed everyone else saw things the same way. I never felt the need to question the light that I saw around others. But Grandma knew, and because of that I now know she was the silent overseer of my gift, a teacher waiting for me to come into the realization that something was different.

I never did understand why she apologized to me for dying. It had never set in with me, though I thought about it often … until a complete stranger walked into my trading post 30 years later and told me what she was seeing.

Truth be told, had it not been for all of the time I spent with my Grandma and Grandpa Rutledge, and my cousins, I'm not sure what would have happened to me. My Aunt Diane also had a very positive impact on my life. I think she felt a little sorry for my sister and I and made it a point to get us out of our stressful home environment. She took me in and taught me how to cook, how to crochet, and how to sew, skills that I still use to this very day. My grandma, my aunt, and my favorite teacher, Miss Blackburn, are the only women I looked up to and respected. They were always kind to me and took an active interest in my wellbeing. Had it not been for their influence on my life, the tale of Two Bears might have been a different kind of story.

CHAPTER 4

Growing Wild

FOR MOST OF my childhood I floated somewhere between happy and sad. We never had a lot, just the bare necessities. We really didn't need a lot either; I guess country folk are just different that way. We got our first TV in 1969. Dad bought it just so we could watch man land on the moon. I figured out early on that if I wanted something I'd have to find a way to get it for myself.

My love for the outdoors and our lack of modern conveniences propelled me into exploring the world outside my door. We lived in the shinnery – a large piece of land thick with scrub Oak trees that grew wild in dense, twisted clumps. It suited me just fine. I ran wild through the shinnery everyday - barefoot and shirtless - tangled, long hair flowing behind me like a wild Indian. The shinnery was my favorite place to be. I understood it somehow and I was comfortable out there. It was nothing but the critters, and the wind, and the feel of the sandy soil beneath my calloused feet.

The shinnery was also my teacher. I learned to track animals and humans out in those woods; I learned to trap and skin the animals I caught. It provided me with my first opportunity at making money.

My first trap was a rusted old Victor Long Spring my uncle had given me. I was so excited when he gave me the trap that I laid awake half the night waiting for daylight. I knew exactly where I was going to set it, and I did, early the next morning before going to school.

I stared at the clock above the classroom door all day and tried to will it to move faster. When, finally, the last bell rang, my cousin Joey and I jumped on our horses and headed out to see if I'd caught anything. Joey was a little off, and in our younger years I was something of his protector. (It wasn't until he became an adult that I would find out just how "off" cousin Joey really was.) But that particular day we saddled up and rode to the spot where I'd set my trap. When we got there, something just wasn't right. My trap wasn't where I'd left it that morning. We dismounted and began scouring the area when I spotted something that looked like rusty metal poking out of a hole a few feet away. Joey and I walked over to investigate. And something hissed.

Figuring that whatever it was was still stuck in the trap, we grabbed the chain and began pulling it out of the hole. Imagine our surprise when out of the hole, tail first, came a big, fat, angry skunk. He was hissing and madder than hell and let us know by spraying a fine mist of green stink all over the both of us. Well, after all the gagging and choking subsided, we set about trying to figure out how to get that skunk out of my trap. After much discussion, we decided to lasso the darned thing, and we drug that poor skunk all over the shinnery until he died. Cruel as that may seem, neither one of us could come up with a better solution.

Although it's fair to say that my first run at trapping was a bit rough, I was never one to give up. I kept at it and, through trial and error, I would eventually become a pretty good trapper. With a few lessons from my grandma I learned to skin and tan the pelts from the animals I trapped and I sold them locally. It put money in my pocket and school clothes on my back.

A Dream Is Born

Now, like most couples who are still honeymooning, my dad and his third wife, Linda, enjoyed going out together with friends and socializing, so I started spending just about every weekend at my Grandma's house. Donna mostly stayed at her best friend's house. But in July of that year, we took our first vacation together as a family. I'll never forget that trip. Dad and I had customized a Good Times van. It was black, complete with shag carpet and fur trim throughout the interior - the Rutledges were traveling in style. We went to Colorado, and as we got closer I could see the silhouette of the San Juan Mountain Range. It didn't even look real to me. I had never seen anything so beautiful, so majestic.

We stayed in Manitou Springs for a couple of nights. While we were there, we took a day trip up Pikes Peak and panned for gold, walked through the Garden of the Gods where the rocks glow red, and went shopping in the stores that lined the streets of Manitou. But it was when we walked through the doors of an old trading post called The Mountain Man Store that my eyes lit up ... and it was there that my dream took root.

We were greeted by a burly, older gentleman wearing fringed buckskin clothes. He had a grizzled look about him but he was the kindest man. My dad lost interest and went outside but I stayed, and I'm pretty sure I touched everything in that store. I felt right at home. The older gentleman took the time to visit with me and was quite impressed with my knowledge of the different species of furs, and how to skin them. He asked my dad if I could stay there with him for the rest of the summer and work in his store. Of course, Dad said no. I was only 10. I was broken hearted. We said our goodbyes and left, but from that very moment, I knew that I wanted to be a mountain man and a trapper. I wanted a trading post where I could sell my skins and wear buckskin shirts and make things from antlers and bear claws. I could see it clearly, but it would be years before I would get close enough to actually touch it.

The Faith of a Child

"Those who are pure in heart, hear the Lord's voice the loudest!"

– *Two Bears*

From the time that I was old enough to read, I spent many hours studying my bible. I had my own; it was a New World version with a green hard cover. I still have that old bible and refer to it often. The margins and pages throughout it are covered with notations and highlighting, all in the handwriting of a child. Verses that, as a young boy, I found to be significant, are jotted down inside the front and back covers.

We attended church on a regular basis, and for some unknown reason, my Dad made the decision that we should become Jehovah's Witnesses. I hated this decision immediately when I discovered that, as Jehovah's Witnesses, we would not be celebrating Christmas, Easter, or even my birthday. Thank goodness my dad discovered early on that were not a good fit with them, and we returned to our traditional Christian worship and beliefs. Those beliefs are what guide me today, as I try to live my life according to God's law over man's law.

I have often wondered why there are so many different religions in the world, and I have come to believe it's because you have imperfect man trying to decipher a perfect law. It's inevitable that everyone's interpretation will vary. That being said, I am a firm believer that we are currently living in Revelations and that Jesus will be returning soon. And from the time I was a little boy, sifting through the pages of wisdom that the Great Spirit provided, I have always felt that it would be the highest honor to be chosen to serve as one of His warriors.

CHAPTER 5

Edumacating

I NEVER TOOK much interest in school and found it some-what boring. In my mind, it was a huge waste of time. Maybe part of the problem was that I was different than the others; I knew it, and so did they. Most of my classmates were involved in sports and partying, but that never appealed to me. When I wasn't in the shinnery, I enjoyed spending my time working, and building things, mostly cars. And while most of the guys I went to school with had short hair, I chose to wear mine long – a choice that brought me more than just ridicule. Ultimately, it resulted in getting me suspended for non-conformity.

Miss Eloise Blackburn

There was one teacher who made school tolerable for me, her name was Miss Eloise Blackburn.

William Arthur Ward, one of America's most quoted writers of inspirational maxims, once wrote: *"The mediocre teacher tells. The good teacher explains. The superior teacher demonstrates. The great teacher inspires."*

Miss Blackburn was a *great* teacher. She taught my dad, she taught me and she taught my oldest daughter, Tori. She was the teacher who put the fire in your ass if you messed up.

Miss Blackburn never married. She told me that she almost got married once, but she never did tell me the whole story, and there were some things that you just didn't ask a woman like Miss Blackburn. Her boundaries were unspoken but there was never any question where they were. She never had any children of her own, but to her we were all her kids.

Miss Blackburn was 5'5" and weighed 170 pounds with dark black hair streaked with grey. She had Native American blood, but I don't know how much. She lived her entire life in a little rock house in Hawley, Texas, and anyone who ever met her will never forget her. She was just that kind of woman.

She taught school for 50 plus years. She made you learn and with that came respect. You didn't buck her. You didn't mess up in her class. You did what you were supposed to do, if you didn't, she'd come along with a ruler and whack you upside the ear. Once was usually all it took. She meant business, everyone knew it, and everyone respected her because of it.

Miss Blackburn didn't care what the history books said. She wasn't afraid to teach the truth and she had an intuitive way of instilling the wonderment of it into our pliable young minds. She taught us how to think for ourselves and was the first one to tell me to look outside the box. She knew that Columbus didn't discover America because the Native Americans were already here. She'd say, "Look for yourself. So, how did he discover anything?"

It is because of Miss Blackburn and her encouragement as a young child that I chased my art and my dreams. At an early age I was drawing and selling pictures. She told me when I was just a little boy, "Son, you have a God given talent and you need to pursue it." I took it to the next level because of her.

Miss Blackburn kept track of me even after I became an adult. Every so often she would call me to tell me how proud of me she was. I made her a pair of hand-stitched moccasins once and she loved them. She wore them every day, and every couple of years she would call me and say, "Mark, this is Eloise. You need to make me another pair of moccasins. I wore these out." And I'd say, "Yes, maam. I'll make them for you." I probably made that woman five pairs of moccasins up until she died three years ago. She never lost track of me and for that I will always be grateful. From the time I was just a little fella sitting in her classroom until the day she died, she made me feel like I mattered.

You can't put a price on the value of a great teacher. They can open your mind and your eyes to the world around you, to life, to the truth and to your own unique talents and abilities.

They can offer you a new perspective regardless of where you come from or the circumstances you live in. They encourage, they inspire, they nurture, but more importantly, they plant seeds. We all have that one *great* teacher that we'll always be thankful for and who we'll never forget. Miss Eloise Blackburn was mine.

But as for the rest of school, I didn't much care. And when they suspended me, it only made my non-conformist attitude that much stronger.

Cowboys and Shears

It was in high school that I had a run in with some cowboys who decided that I was in need of a haircut. I was sitting on the hood of my '67 Ford Fastback Mustang that I'd just built, eating lunch, when Dana, a friend from school, came running over to give me the heads up that three guys were coming my way and they intended to cut my hair with sheep shears. I quickly looked around for anything I could use to defend myself and found a wooden bed slat laying in the dirt. I tucked it under my leg and waited. When the cowboys rounded the corner and saw me, they were cocky and ready to rumble. "Hey, hippie," they shouted. "Guess what. We're fixing to cut your hair." Calmly, I advised them that they might not want to do that … and it was on. The leader with the shears lunged at me, but before he knew what hit him, I smacked him upside the head with that bed slat. The bed slat turned out to be a pretty good equalizer. I was able to quickly turn and disable the second guy. And the third, well, he took off in a dead run, so just to make sure I got my point across, I chased him down and whacked him across the back. It was the pursuit of that third buckaroo that resulted in my week long suspension from school, which I spent without having lost a single strand of my long hair.

But that wasn't the first time I'd been suspended from school. My dad always commissioned me with the responsibility of watching out for my older sister. On this particular day my sister and I were riding home on the school bus. For no good reason (other than he was a jerk) my cousin Joey started picking on my sister Donna and he just wouldn't quit. Because it was my duty to protect her, I stood up and told him that he'd best quit messing with her. Joey, being the antagonist that he was, responded, "Oh yeah? What are you going to do about it?" So, in an effort to make myself clear, I grabbed him by the collar with one hand, and by his belt with the other, and shoved him face first out an open window. It was my intent to stuff him completely out the window and on to the street when Mr. Ed, the bus driver, saw what was happening. He slammed on the brakes, kicked me off the bus, and promptly left me there on the side of the road. Looking back, I guess it was a good thing that Joey's big old belt buckle got hung up on the window. Falling out of the window while the bus was moving might've killed him. And, of course, once the principal heard about the incident, I was placed on suspension. There was one good thing that came from it, though. When I walked down the hallways after I served my time and was allowed back to school, it was like Moses parting the Red Sea. You can rest assured from that day forward, he, nor anybody else ever showed any disrespect to my sister.

Cousin Joey

It was during our teenage years when the true depth of my cousin Joey's insanity became clear. We were in class one day and Joey was being his usual disruptive self, cutting up and making a scene with total disregard to the rules. Our teacher was sitting at her desk filing her fingernails with one of the old metal fingernail files ladies used back then. She told Joey to sit down and be quiet. As usual, he completely ignored her and continued with his antics. I suspect he'd finally gotten on her last nerve because she stood up, slammed her hands down on the desk, and yelled, "Look you little retard! I told you to sit down and be quiet!!" The classroom fell silent. And while we all sat there in disbelief, Joey stood up, walked over to her desk, grabbed that metal fingernail file out from between her fingers, and stabbed it right through her hand and into the desk. That poor woman let out one hell of a blood curdling scream that could be heard throughout the entire school.

That was the end of Joey's high school career. To say his cheese had slid off his cracker was an understatement - the kid was certifiably crazy. A few years later Joey was sentenced to life in prison with no possibility of parole for caving in the head of a young lady with a rock and throwing her lifeless body into Lake Fort Phantom. Ironically, several years later I would end up working this case with my task force partner when the body was finally discovered.

The Right Stuff

As my senior year approached, many of my fellow classmates already had plans for after graduation. Some were going off to college, and some of the athletes received scholarships and had been recruited by universities. There wasn't any college money for me, or scholarships coming my way, and I didn't really have any plans. I was never the kid who had dreams of becoming a doctor or lawyer when I grew up. I did, however, have the opportunity to enlist in the military. I will never forget the Saturday morning that military recruiters from every branch of the service knocked on my dad's door. They told me that based on my standard aptitude test scores, I had "the stuff" they were looking for. They tried enticing me with promises of advanced ranking upon enlistment. Whether it was that my dad had other plans for me, or whether it was because of his own experiences in the Army, I don't know, but he abruptly stood up and told the recruiters, "Thank you for your interest in my son. Now, I believe it's time for you all to be leaving.' I have often wondered what my life would be like now, had I enlisted.

CHAPTER **6**

Street Rods and Motorcycles

When I was about 14, I decided I wanted to build my very own street rod, so my cousin Danny and I started cruising through the shinnery searching for old cars. You could usually find an old car or two hiding in tall grass in a farmer's field. We spotted a '29 Chevrolet on an old farm in Funston. It was sitting in the farmer's backyard wrapped with chicken wire and was being used as a chicken coop. I asked the old man if he'd be interested in selling it to me and he asked me what I had to offer. I had a total of $100 in my pocket. He said that wasn't enough and asked if I had any guns. I had an old 16 gauge shotgun that I used to hunt birds, and because it wasn't the greatest gun I owned, I didn't mind putting it on the table as part of my offer. The deal was made.

Danny and I loaded the rusty frame in the back of his pick up and hauled it home. When we arrived, my dad asked me what I was going to do with it. I proudly told him I was going to build a street rod. He hesitated for a moment, and as he walked away I heard him say, "Sure you are". He went on to add that he would not be helping me in any way other than to supervise. With what I earned as a stock boy after school and on weekends working at the Super Duper grocery store, I had managed to save a little bit of money. I would go parts shopping with my meager savings at the FM600 wrecking yard. When I wasn't working at the Super Duper, I worked on that car afterschool and on weekends for almost two years. And when I finished it, I drove it to school.

There is nothing more rewarding than succeeding at something someone else said you couldn't do. Through the years I upgraded and improved that car, and I kept it until I decided to move to New Mexico almost 30 years later. I didn't want to sell it, but I needed the cash to carry me on the last leg of my journey towards my dream. That street rod was the first of many cars I would build, including a '67 Ford Fastback Mustang.

I also built a 1975 Camaro. It was yellow with orange flames coming up the hood. Late one night I was coming home from work, and as was the norm, I was hauling ass. A DPS trooper got in behind me with his lights flashing. I was tired and really didn't feel like getting a ticket that night, so I put my foot into the accelerator and left him like he was sitting still. The next day at school, while sitting in Miss Blackburn's class, that DPS officer paid me a visit. I may have outrun him the night before but I still got that darned ticket. He knew me and he knew my car. Just goes to prove that you can only outrun the law for a little while, but eventually they'll catch up to you.

Two Wheels and Riding the Wind

My passion for motorcycles was born at a young age. I was seven years old when Dad decided he had to have one. The only thing I knew for sure was that if Dad was going to have one, so would I. And Dad knew me well enough to understand that. So, with me working right alongside him, together we built me my very own chopper mini bike.

We constructed the frame out of one-inch steel tubing and put a 5 horse power Briggs and Stratton engine on it. We shined her up and painted it gold. It was the coolest thing I'd ever had and it was mine!

I got my first ticket on that mini bike. Well, actually, my mom got the ticket. I was out one afternoon, riding somewhere that I shouldn't have been, driving faster than I should've been and when a police officer tried to stop me, I flipped him the bird and kept on going. I thought I was invincible. After all, I'd had grandpa as a teacher.

In that small town everybody knew everybody, and, of course, the police officer knew who I was and where I lived. He beat me home and issued a citation to my mom. Needless to say, she was none too happy when I finally rolled in.

But I was hooked. Since then, I have had a love for motorcycles and have never been without one.

That memory is one of the dearest I have of my dad. We had such a good time working together on that bike. More importantly, it made a young boy feel like a man.

The Road to Responsibility

That street rod also carried me to another phase of my life. The popular thing to do during my teenage years was to cruise North 1st street in Abilene. From one end to the other, a parade of cars would cruise back and forth, occasionally joining together in nearby parking lots where we'd hang out and do what teenagers do. It was during a night of cruising that I met Paige, who I would eventually marry and have two daughters with. I was sixteen years old and had already begun building a house on a piece of land adjacent to my father's home. I bought the land with money I'd saved from my job at the grocery store and what I made selling my skins.

Saving that money was no easy task. I got the job at the Super Duper when I was 14 years old and my father immediately demanded that I start paying rent. By then he had married his third wife, Linda, and at that time, I think she would have preferred that I wasn't there at all. I'd sit in my room at night and draw up plans for the house I wanted to build. When the opportunity came along to buy the land from my uncle, I jumped at it.

I'd set my traps in the mornings before school. When the school day was over, I'd head home and check my traps, then head off to work at the grocery store. Any time I had free, I spent working on my house. Little by little I'd buy what materials I couldn't cultivate on my own. And every payday my father would be waiting at the door with his hand out demanding the rent. I finally got tired of it and moved in with Paige at her mother's house. Minimum wage only stretched so far. I split my time between Paige's house and dad's house until I graduated.

Part Two
Somewhere in Between

CHAPTER 1

Hunting and Shenanigans

IT WAS DURING that time, right after I graduated, that I landed a job working for a hot oil transport company. It was just a job, nothing I had ever hoped or aspired to excel in – just a paycheck. To break up our boring, mundane days it wasn't uncommon to entertain ourselves by pulling pranks on our buddies. My good friend Larry worked there with me, and Larry had an extreme phobia of snakes. Well, one of the guys had caught himself a rattlesnake and the opportunity to mess with Larry was too good to pass up. I took the snake and wired his mouth closed with a piece of bailing wire and put it under the seat of Larry's transport truck.

Larry arrived at work that morning and, like he always did, said his hellos, got himself some coffee, and checked his route for the day. Ready to hit the road, he headed over to his truck and loaded up. We watched as he started his engine, put the truck in gear, and drove away. He only made it about 200 yards. From the doorway of the shop, we watched the door of his truck fly open and Larry come sailing out like a self-propelled rocket, tripping and flailing. Off he went, rolling across the field, cussing and a screaming. It was more than that poor dude could handle when he realized it was a rattlesnake that was striking the back of his leg. The truck – well, it was still rolling too. Fortunately, the engine died as it crossed into a bar ditch or we'd have all lost our jobs.

The next time I was with Larry and we saw a snake, we were out hunting arrowheads, something we enjoyed and frequently did together. He pulled his gun on me, promising to shoot me if I went anywhere near the damn thing. I believed him.

In 2001, Larry was elected as sheriff of Jones County, and he still serves as sheriff today. He is the epitome of a true and honest man, kind and gentle. More importantly, he's also the one man you know would not leave your side during a shootout. I'm proud to call him my friend.

Hunts with Marvin

Paige and I married when I was 18 years old, and even though the house wasn't finished yet, we moved in. It took me three years to finally complete and we struggled financially. It seemed like I could never make enough money to cover our obligations, much less buy diapers and formula to feed the babies when they came along. We had two daughters, Tori and Shelbi, eight years apart. More often than not I worked two or three jobs in an effort to provide for my family.

We weren't ready, but at 21 our first child arrived. I brought Tori home in a 1969 Stingray Corvette I had built. We were struggling. At that time I was working for my dad and was out of town a lot. I knew a baby was going to change my life drastically. I picked up side jobs here and there to earn some extra cash.

One of my favorite side jobs was hog hunting. To call it "hunting" really isn't accurate – hog eradicating is far more fitting.

Area farmers had a terrible problem with wild hogs tearing up their fields and destroying their crops. They say that the hog population in Texas is over 2 million strong and is experiencing a 21 percent growth rate every year. Damage done by feral hogs is estimated at $52 million annually. Farmers take an aggressive approach to control and protect their investments by hiring individuals to hunt or trap these destructive beasts.

I easily made more money on the weekends hunting hogs than I did from my regular job. When the evening would roll around, I would head out to a farmer's field and sit on the hood of my Chevy truck, where I would wait patiently in the dark for the hogs to start moving in. You could always hear them coming, and I would wait, letting them surround me. Then I would flip on my K.C. lights and start firing away. Hogs aren't real smart as they'd scatter when the gun fired, but when the lights went back off, they'd come right back. So, I'd flip the lights off, and do it again. I got paid around $10.00 per hog, and it was nothing for me to kill 50 per night.

Hunting was always a favorite activity for me, whether it was a chance to put some meat on the table or an opportunity to earn a little extra cash. Along with Marvin, one of my closest friends, I got involved in some 24-hour predator hunting contests that were hosted locally. During those hunts, you and your teammate were allowed to hunt predators like coyotes, fox, bobcat, etc. for a 24 hour period. At the end of the 24 hours, all participants returned to the hosting company to turn in their catch. Prize money was awarded based on quantity of kills, the biggest coyote, the biggest bobcat, and so on.

Marvin and I were a great team, often winning all categories. On one memorable weekend, Marvin decided to bring his 8 year old son Dawson along for the ride. That night we had permission to hunt on a friend's ranch that was somewhat familiar to us, so we loaded up and went out patrolling the fields. Since most of the hunt took place in the dark, the use of predator calls and spotlights were necessary.

We got on a pack of dogs and Marvin floored his truck, chasing after them across that wheat field. We were in hot pursuit of those coyotes, sliding sideways, back and forth across the rough terrain. I was hanging out the window with my 12 gauge in hand while Marvin tried to keep the truck on four wheels. Caught up in the excitement of the chase, neither Marvin nor I remembered that Dawson was in the back of the truck. That boy was being tossed around like a rag doll and we were oblivious to it. But when the chase finally subsided, he let his presence be known. He surfaced from the floorboard, laughing so hard he could barely talk, screaming, "Hot Damn! That was AWESOME!!!" Another adrenaline junkie was born that night.

On another weekend predator hunt, Marvin and I were cruising around in the fields looking for coyotes when we noticed an all too familiar odor that both of us knew to be associated with the cooking of methamphetamine. Spotting the old, run down farmhouse that the stench was emanating from, we called in to the Taylor County Task Force and requested assistance. When back-up arrived we entered the house on a no-knock entry, catching a 19 year old kid cooking a batch of meth. Turns out he was using stolen anhydrous ammonia. The task force agents made the arrest and took him away to jail and a clean-up crew was dispatched to the property to clean up and dispose of the hazardous materials. The kid lived with his grandfather. The weathered old man, who appeared to be in his 80's, had been suffering abuse at the hands of his grandson. Over and over the old man expressed his gratitude to us for saving his life. Little did I know the scenario would become one I would be intimately familiar with in the not so distant future.

Marvin and I jumped on just about any opportunity we had to go hunting. One year, we got the opportunity to go elk hunting in Cuchara, Colorado with a couple of friends named Terry and Hank. Cuchara is high in the southern Colorado Rockies, and Trinchera Peak, one of Colorado's 300 highest peaks, rises majestically above the Sangre De Cristo mountain range. It is truly beautiful country and provides some fantastic hunting. Marvin, Terry, and I were all seasoned hunters and outdoor enthusiasts. We were what Hank wanted to be.

It wasn't long before we realized that Hank was not as experienced as we originally thought, or that he'd led on to be. He clearly was uncomfortable in the wilderness, afraid to split up and go out alone for fear of getting lost. His anxiety presented us with some good pranking opportunities and poor Hank – we broke him in good.

One night during the trip the temperature dropped down in to the low teens. It was cold and we were all ready to call it good and retire for the evening. Marvin had an old heavy metal boat anchor lying in the bed of his truck, so while Hank was going through his 20 minute pre-bedtime routine, we decided to tuck it down into the foot of his sleeping bag. When he finally crawled into his bed and his feet hit that frozen anchor he damned near tore the RV up trying to get out of it. Marvin, Terry, and I roared with laughter. But we weren't satisfied.

The next morning, while Hank was taking care of business in the outhouse, Marvin and I hid under the tongue of the RV. We could hear Hank tromping through the forest on his way back, and as he reached the edge of our campsite, Marvin fired a few rounds at his feet. I can tell you that seeing Hank, in his boxers, his hunting boots, and his cowboy hat doing the Fred Flintstone shuffle is just about one of the funniest things I've ever seen.

Hank is, without a doubt, one of the best natured, jolliest guys I have ever known, and I am so thankful that he can take a joke. Hank has since became a good hunter, has bagged a few elk and deer as of late, and to this day is a friend and fellow Harley rider! Marvin also remains one of my dearest and best friends to this day.

The Tarantula and the Toilet Brush

As time went on, I finally landed a good job as a welder with General Dynamics in Abilene. It was a God send.

While I worked there, I was presented with yet another opportunity to pull a prank, this time on one of my co-workers. It's really not that I am always trying to scare the crap out of my friends, but far be it from me to pass up a good opportunity when one presents itself. This time my target was a fella named Randy Scott. Randy was a behemoth of a man, standing at 7' 2", who'd had a promising future with the NBA until he blew his knee out.

Now, everyone knows that most colored folks are scared of spiders and snakes, and despite his size, Randy was no exception. I'd stumbled upon a wooden box one day that had a spring loaded hinge on it -and my wheels were turning. I decided it would be great fun to tie the head of a black toilet bowl brush to the hinge, giving it an eerie resemblance to a tarantula. Holding the box up close to myself, I could hit a trip lever making the "tarantula" suddenly spring out.

Everyone was gathered around me when Randy walked in, and seeing the group huddled together, his curiosity was piqued. He looked at the box and then he looked at me and asked what I had in the box. I told him I'd caught a tarantula. "Come look," I said. I tried to ease his apprehension by assuring him that it was contained. At that time, Randy had no reason to doubt me, so he cautiously moved in closer to investigate. I held the box out and tapped on the sides, as if to knock the spider around so Randy could get a better view of it, and because he couldn't see it, he leaned in closer. That's when I hit the trip lever, and BAM! - out of the box and into Randy's face went that black brush. Randy let out a scream that I'm almost certain the whole plant heard, and in one swift move, jumped over the break room table, arms flailing about, trying to knock off the spider that he knew was on him - and he kept on running, full speed, out of the room. When he came back, we were all still rolling with laughter. Randy told me "Mark, you must clank when you walk!" ; He'd never met a braver man.

Randy Scott is a strong Christian man with a very humble heart, and has been blessed with a beautiful family. I love this man and would give him the shirt off my back.

It was because of the decent pay and working with good men like Randy that I enjoyed my years working at General Dynamics, aka "the plant," yet all the while I had a longing desire to be in the mountains. I'd sketched a picture of a log cabin when I was ten or eleven years old that I had envisioned in my head. I could see it as clearly as I'd ever seen anything and I dreamed about one day building it high atop a mountain, surrounded by nothing but forest, where I could live life on my terms. I put the drawing in an old, wooden frame and throughout the years I kept it displayed prominently where I could see it. I could see the life I wanted in that pencil sketch and it called to me continuously, like the echo of wolves howling in the distance. But with all of the financial struggles and a young family to provide for, I just didn't know how I would ever get there. And Paige showed little interest in my dream.

My thirst for adventure, and a handful of friends who shared that spirit, sustained me through those years. It was then that I would also discover the Mountain Man Rendezvous – a gathering of folks who take great pleasure in reenacting the days of the beaver fur trade era that took place during the early part of the 1800's.

CHAPTER **2**

Birds of a Feather

I ATTENDED MY first mountain man rendezvous in 1980. I'd heard about them around the time a friend of mine and I were going up into the mountains to trap beaver. Always looking to make extra money, my friend and I thought we'd get in on it and make a little extra cash. Heck, we were just doing what we loved anyway.

I'm not sure who first told me about the rendezvous; it may have been him. But the crux of it is this: The mountain man rendezvous came about when there was a need to resupply the fur traders in the early part of the 1800s. It was 1820 and the demand for beaver fur was high. The well to do Europeans found the stove-pipe top hats to be a status symbol, and the top hats were made with beaver fur. By 1840 it had dwindled down to nothing, but for that 20 year reign, life was good for the mountain man trappers. It's that 20 year reign that the mountain man rendezvous recaptures.

The mountain man rendezvous encampments follow strict criteria. Everything in the camp is required to be pre-1840s including your attire and your gear. Everything has to be handmade, hand sewn and period correct.

For many years it was an extremely popular reenactment movement, but the group took a hit when the Single Action Shooter Society, a cowboy reenactment group, was formed. Many folks were drawn to the SASS society because it was more modern. You could shoot proper ammo, not just black powder rifles and the overall criteria were less stringent. But today, with the cost of bullets and powder rising, less people are joining SASS and many are returning to the mountain man rendezvous'.

Scouting Out the Territory

I attended my very first rendezvous, the Fort Phantom Rendezvous in Abilene, in 1980. I chose the Fort Phantom Rendezvous as my first look into the group for obvious reasons. First, it was close to home and, second, it was open to the public on the weekends.

I spent the weekend visiting with the men at the encampment and learning from them. These guys are very intelligent when it comes to this. They know the laws and the way it was – pointblank, they know their history. And so you go around these old men at these rendezvous' and just let them talk to you. You wear buckskin clothing and take the time to sit around the campfire and drink whiskey with them, listen to their stories and cook on the open flame. It was a natural fit and I was hooked.

Nineteen-eighty-two was the first year I actually participated in a rendezvous. Since then I've been to hundreds of them. Most are held in the spring, summer and fall but there are some that happen even in the dead of winter. And they're not exclusive to the U.S. Folks from all over the world participate, and many of them travel from as far away as Belgium and Germany, using their vacation time to come and experience a different lifestyle for a few weeks each year.

Days are spent horseback riding, fishing, hiking or doing whatever you want to do. Competitions are big throughout the rendezvous with daily offerings of muzzleloader shoots, tomahawk competitions, knife throwing contests, primitive bow shoots, pie contests, cooking contests and the like.

Traders are abundant, selling everything from hand-stitched clothing to homemade knives to hand bound leather journals with homemade paper. Some of the guys that were traders at Fort Phantom Rendezvous I visited in Abilene in 1980 are still traders at the rendezvous' today.

If you're gonna camp you have to pay, because they supply water and ice and firewood. It usually costs my rendezvous partner and I $100 bill to stay for two weeks at rendezvous – not bad for two weeks dirt rental, water and a warm fire. A good number of the folks come with teepees. Some come with wedge tents or baker's tents. Most of the younger fellas start out with teepee's but they're a pain in the ass to load and unload, so most of the guys, as they get older, will sell their teepee and get something small that they can handle on their own. A lot of these guys are up in age and they just hit the rendezvous circuit. They buy, sell and trade one to the other all over the country.

It is fairly expensive to get started in. You have to have buckskin clothes and period-correct costumes. You can't walk around inside the rendezvous in your street clothes on weekdays. But on weekends when it's open to the public you can wear whatever you want, and go by the different tents and trade and hang out and visit with everyone. When it's open to the public all rules are off. Then Monday through Friday it's back on again, pre-1840s everything – right down to your cooking utensils and the stitching in your boots.

It's Who You Are

Rendezvous folk are a close knit group. Some of my closest friendships have been formed at rendezvous. Friends made there are lifelong. It's a group of people who are drawn like a moth to a flame - to a simpler, but not necessarily easier time. Word gets around fast and troublemakers or untrustworthy folks are not welcomed back.

We have one guy, his camp name is Just Josh, who brings his young daughter with him to rendezvous every year. His daughter has her own camp name; Pixie Dust. One year Just Josh had to leave the rendezvous for a few days to take care of some work related issues. Josh told Pixie Dust, "If you get hungry, go over to Two Bears tent and he'll make sure you get something to eat.' It made me feel good that he trusted me enough to take care of his little girl, but he also knew that I raised two girls of my own. He said that rendezvous was the only place he felt comfortable letting his kids just run wild, with no supervision whatsoever from him. Everyone there looks out after your kid - everyone. And it's not unusual to see hundreds of them running all over the place, in period dress and costume. The kids have a blast. And if anyone tried to harm a little one, they'd have a whole camp on them in the blink of an eye.

At Rendezvous you won't find any cellphones, or TV's, no headphones, and no IPads. The only music you hear is at night, live around the glow of a campfire – banjos, guitars, harmonicas and flutes. Even the music is period correct - and a lot of dancing, picking and grinning and whiskey drinking accompanies it.

I look forward to rendezvous every year. I have a ball there. I can just cut loose, be myself, and don't have to try to impress anybody - we do what we want to do, and no one really cares.

Many women rendezvous too. You'll see women ranging in age from 13 to 70 years old. Bones, a woman that is a regular, is a friend of mine. She's a hell of a shot. She's comes out there by herself, brings her own clothing, her own tent, her own guns, she does it all by herself. No husband, no boyfriend, no nothing. Ornery as she can be.

There's another little gal we named Doe Eyes. She turned 21 while she was at rendezvous and got drunk at the Turtle, the camp saloon. Me and another fella scooped her up and carried her out to her camp and put her in her tent. We named her Doe Eyes because her eyes were all glossed over. She's a regular too, and I love her to death. I've met so many buck skinners like Bobcat, Slayer, Taylor, No nose , Wild Bill; there are just too many to write down here in this book, it would take up ten pages, but know that I didn't forget you and love you all the same..

You honestly never know who you'll meet at rendezvous. Two good friends that I met a few years back are Tom Oar and Will Stringfellow from the History Channel show 'The Mountain Men.' Guaranteed you'll never meet two finer true-to-life mountain men than these fellows. Barbra and I have vacationed at Tom's place and we sell Tom and Will's pelts in the trading post. They, too, are traders living life on their own terms.

I set up shop at rendezvous on Trader's Row, which is where

I met Tom and Will. I'm a trader. I sell my creations to rendezvous visitors when I'm there, but since opening Two Bears Trading Post I usually buy more than I sell. I have found that I can get better deals on stuff there than I can anywhere else. I haul it back to my store and sell it to the public, so it doubles as a good avenue for generating income.

My wife, Barbra, goes sometimes, too. She has her own buckskin dresses and everything she needs, but a lot of times rendezvous falls during busy times at the trading post, and one of us needs to be there to man the shop.

I quit going for ten years when I started Two Bears Trading Post. I had to train Barbra to make sure she knew what to do, how to do it; how to wheel and deal. But now – heck, she can do it just as good as I can. That frees me up, allowing me to go. We fill the store up with what I bring home. If something I've brought in to the store isn't selling, I'll load it up and take it to the next rendezvous, trading for something different.

These days, my rendezvous partner is Jason, camp name Scout. He's a quiet man of few words and the kind of fellow you know you can trust right away. He's very smart and when he does speak, you listen. And best of all - he doesn't snore!

Word gets around camp about who you are. To be honest with you, I really don't think anyone at camp even knows my real name. To them, I am Two Bears. They know me, and they know my story and they know what I'm all about. They also know I'm a fair dealer and there's no bullshit with me. I do the deal and I take care of it.

You get to know people pretty well and most of the people that go to the rendezvous' are just good-hearted folks born 150 years too late. That's why I fit in – because that's what I've been accused of all my life and that's alright by me. I have a favorite saying that came to me many years ago that holds true today.

"You laugh at me because I'm different. I laugh at you because you are all the same."

- Two Bears

CHAPTER 3

Adventures Above and Below Sea Level

IF IT HADN'T been for a handful of kindred spirits hell bent on adventure to help break up the monotony of the day-to-day grind - and ease the stress of struggling to provide for a young family - I'd like to have gone out of my mind. Here are just a few of those adventures.

Hiking the Tetons

I was working for General Dynamics in Abilene in 1992 before Lockheed bought them out, and a group of guys decided they wanted to hike the Grand Tetons. Always up for an adventure, I signed on quick. There were six of us – me, a friend named Mike, the local district attorney and three others.

My friend Mike weighed 150 pounds soaking wet and was headstrong as hell. I loved him to death, but this would be just one of several times I wanted to throw him off a cliff.

The district attorney had his own airplane. He, Mike and I flew to Wyoming – his plane wasn't big enough to carry all of us with our gear so the other three guys drove up and met us there.

When we arrived at the airport, we collected our gear and rented a taxi to Jenny Lake, then rented a boat to cross the lake to the trailhead. Mike was supposed to be my partner. He got altitude sickness right from the start. We hadn't been there 30 minutes and he was throwing up.

I went up ahead a little ways. Mike waited for about an hour or so and was finally able to gain his composure and catch up with us. Fortunately he was fine the rest of the trip, at least as far as altitude sickness was concerned. One problem solved.

When we stopped to camp for the night, Mike was determined to build a snow cave. He was sure it would keep him warmer. He liked to have froze his ass off.

A couple days in we found ourselves hiking a trail with 14

feet of snow underfoot – a potentially dangerous situation. I told everyone that we needed to put our snowshoes on so we didn't fall through. Mike didn't want to put them on. He was in the lead on the trail. There was no reasoning with him.

The rest of us strapped on our snowshoes and continued down the trail behind Mike, when instantly, like he'd stepped into a suction powered vortex, Mike vanished. Sure enough, the mule-headed fool had fallen through the snow. It seemed like forever before he hit the ground 14 feet below. I inched toward the hole where he'd fallen and peered over. I could see his face looking up at me, the rest of his body buried in snow.

The five of us went into instant panic mode. I threw off my pack and grabbed my climbing rope and threw it down to him. Mike managed to dig out around himself enough to secure the rope around his waist.

You'd think it would be easy for five strong guys to lift out 150 pounds, but it wasn't. We were buried up to our knees with snow shoes on. We like to have not gotten his ass out of there. That's how people die. But slowly we managed to hoist him up and get him out.

Once we determined that he was okay, everyone had a few choice words for Mike.

Mike put his snow shoes on after that.

In all we hiked hundreds of miles over the course of two weeks' time, conquering the Grand Tetons with no further incidents. When we reached the bottom at Jackson Hole, we rented a motel room. All of us were longing for a hot shower and a good meal. I lost 14 pounds during that trip.

It wouldn't be the last big adventure with Mike that could have cost someone their life. The next time would be 105 feet underwater, and the life in jeopardy would be mine.

Tales from the Deep

I love scuba diving. Mike and I took classes on Saturdays, and along with my buddy Terry, and a guy from class named Chip, we spent many weekends in the murky waters of Texas lakes.

Eventually all of us became certified divers and Chip and I went as far as getting our dive instructor permits. Chip and I dove a lot and one day Chip made a phone call to Carnival Cruise Lines. They were looking for dive instructors to teach passengers on the boat. Chip sent a picture of the two of us, and shortly after a lady from the cruise line called and asked what it would take to get us as a team. Unfortunately, I was married at the time and my wife wouldn't let me, but I can't say that I blame her. I was in my 20's and Chip looked like he could've been a member of the Chippendales. It was the makings for trouble.

Chip took the job and stayed on the boat for months. Last I'd heard he'd taken a job in Florida on the beach with a dive shack.

I don't get to dive much anymore, but during that time of my life, my buddies and I went on many an adventure on and under the water. Here are a couple highlights.

The Cave

Every chance we got, Mike, Terry, and I went scuba diving at Lake Amstead in Del Rio, Texas. This particular day began like most of our trips - we were hyped up and ready to get in the water. We geared up and jumped in feet first.

We were diving near the bluffs at Lake Amstead on the Mexican border, and the further we descended, the murkier the water became. It wasn't long before you couldn't see your hand in front of your face.

Now, 100 feet is your safe dive limit. When I finally hit the bottom, I pulled my regulator up to check my depth gauge and saw that I was at 105 feet, which is pushing it. I decided that was far enough.

I couldn't find Mike or Terry or another guy that was with us because the water was so murky. One of the number one rules in diving is if you lose your dive partner, you're sup-posed to head to the surface – resurface, regroup and find where everyone is, so that's what I decided to do. But when I tried to go up, I slammed head first into a rock.

It took me a minute to gather my thoughts. I didn't realize that what I'd done was descended feet first directly into a cave. I couldn't see anything so I pulled out my flashlight and started shining it around trying to get my bearings. I could see the rock above my head and thought that I'd drifted under a ledge or something.

I tried to feel along the ledge with my hands because there's an undertow that will pull you out into the lake. But I couldn't find the hole that I came in through and I couldn't find the edge of the cliff.

For the first time in my life, I thought I was going to drown and I started to panic. I remember thinking I had just screwed up royally. Then I got to thinking Mike would be trying to find me. But deep down I knew he was off doing his own thing. He's Mike and he thinks he's bullet proof. For him, the rules don't apply. Finally, I gathered my wits about me, tried to keep calm and slowed my breathing down so I could control my air.

When I exhaled I pulled my regulator out and blew my buoyancy compensator up so I would float, and I felt myself hit that ceiling. I was stuck on the roof of this cave on my hands and knees. Doing everything I could to keep calm, I exhaled, shined my light on the air bubbles and followed them.

The first time I followed them they led me to a hole that was about big enough to put my head in but nothing else. I crawled away from that hole and exhaled again. Finally, after what seemed like an eternity, I saw the air bubbles going off to the left and followed them. Sure enough, there was the hole I'd come in through.

I got to about 30 feet and dumped my air to decompress. I had to be there for ten minutes. I stared at my watch and I could see my air was running out. After making it out of the cave, there was no way I wasn't getting to the surface. I started really controlling my breathing, slowing it way down, and finally made it to the surface.

I bobbed up and down on the surface in the middle of the lake for about ten minutes and finally Mike and Terry and the other dude bobbed up. It was the first time in my life I thought I was a dead man.

The Grouper and the Deep Blue Sea

"It is far more important to be aware of a single shortcoming in ourselves than it is to be aware of a thousand in somebody else"

– Dalai Lama

One January some friends and I made plans to take a diving trip to Cozumel. We were leaving the following week and my good friend Terry wanted to go. But he wasn't certified yet. Our scuba instructor, Walt, said he would certify Terry but said we'd need to meet him at Possum Kingdom Lake right outside of Abilene.

The day we met Walt at the lake it was sleeting and snowing. Walt was the only one with a dry suit – he could blow it up with air so the cold water wouldn't touch his skin. We had wet suits, which was unfortunate. We poured hot water down our wet suits and completely froze when we jumped in that lake. We were shivering cold but we had to get it done, and we did, but we nearly froze our asses off.

This would be my first time in the ocean and the first time I'd actually be able to see a long way underwater. The only diving I'd ever done was in lakes with low visibility. I was in my early twenties and adventurous as hell. When we arrived in Cozumel, I couldn't wait.

The next day we were on the boat and ready to go. I was the first to gear up and the dive instructor told me to go ahead and get in the water and get ready. I had all of my gear on, rolled off the boat and closed my eyes, but I was sinking immediately. I didn't know that salt water was more buoyant than fresh water and my weight belt had too much weight on it. But that didn't panic me. I knew I could just hit the button and add air to my buoyancy control vest and I'd head right back up to the surface. But as soon as I opened my eyes, no further than 50 feet in front of me was a big, black Grouper. He was as big as a Volkswagen and his eyes were as big as five gallon buckets. I looked at him and he looked back at me like I was lunch.

Under water everything looks ten percent larger than life, so you can just imagine how big this fish looked to me. I'm thinking, "Oh, shit." I felt like a Tic Tac to Moby Dick out there. I didn't think twice. I pumped that buoyancy compensator up and I was just a-kicking heading for the surface. I grabbed the ramp on the stern and practically flew back onto that boat.

The dive master, a little Spanish guy, looked at me and asked what was wrong. I told him there was a fish down there big enough to eat me. Everyone got hysterical laughing. They'd never seen me turn that white before.

The Murky Underworld

My scuba and rescue dive certification also opened up a new means for making money. I was often called upon to help solve cases of vehicle theft and perform cadaver searching in Fort Phantom Lake.

The first time I was called out was to search for a man who the authorities suspected had drowned in the lake. Now, Fort Phantom Lake is one of the murkiest lakes I've ever been in. And when I dove in, it was so murky I literally could not see my hand in front of my face. Running my hands blindly across the bottom surface of the lake was my only option. I finally came across what I believed to be a body and was prepared to surface with it, but when I came up, all I had was an arm.

Up, Up, and Away

When we weren't scuba diving Terry had a 21 foot boot and we'd go parasailing. It always attracts a crowd.

The wind was blowing pretty good that day – close to 40 mph. Mike was getting the chute ready, I was in the harness, and Terry was in the boat. Terry and Mike were in control of my destiny. Terry shouted that he was ready. Mike popped the chute up, it caught the puff of wind, and Terry gave it the gas. Usually you have to take a few steps to go. Not that day. It jerked me clean out of my tennis shoes and catapulted me 500 feet in the air in a millisecond.

Terry dropped me on shore, and Mike was fixing to harness up. There was a drunk hippie who'd wandered over with his girlfriend and he was mouthing off about how we were doing everything wrong. He would not shut up. Finally I asked him, "You want to get on this thing and show us how to do it?" well of course he did.

So we put him in the harness and he started shouting orders. Mike and I yelled to Terry to go for it. Now, Terry's jet boat had a big block Chevy engine in it, a bad ass boat. The hippie's yelling at Terry to give it full gas. Terry hit the gas, the chute didn't open and the wind blew it to the rocks. The hippie hit the rocks face first, got dragged across the rocks and hit the water down below.

When we pulled him up, he'd blackened both his eyes, busted his nose, his knees and everything else. He was a bloody mess. But this dumb ass wanted to do it again. This time, he says, don't give it so much gas. We harnessed him up again, shaking our heads. Terry hit the gas, and off the cliff the drunk idiot went again. He wouldn't listen to anybody. He wanted to do it again, to "show us how it was really done". Terry had had enough. "Forget it," he said. "I'm tired of dragging this dumb ass off the cliff."

A Change in Direction

Those adventures all took place during the years I worked at General Dynamics, and I probably would have stayed working there, but when Lockheed Martin bought General Dynamics they threatened that if the union was voted in, they would shut the Abilene plant down. Sure enough, the union was voted in and the plant was shut down, laying off hundreds of highly skilled employees

Unions were good in their day. They had a place and a time and they served a purpose, but I believe the effectiveness of unions has long since passed. At any rate, things happen for a reason and it's because I got laid off from the plant that I decided on a career change that would alter every aspect of my life in a profound and dramatic way. I decided to enroll in the police academy to pursue a career in law enforcement.

"No free man shall ever be debarred the use of arms"

- Thomas Jefferson

Part Three
The Badge

CHAPTER 1

Introduction

POLICE - THE most educated idiots on the street. Thousands of hours spent at schools, and training, and certifications and all to gain employment in a field that promises some of the lowest wages. For the amount of time you spend in training, you could attend college and become a lawyer earning real money. So, why make this career choice? Most of us enter into law enforcement with the hopes and aspirations of making a difference. Unfortunately it doesn't take long to realize that, as a police officer, you are but a grain of sand in a sea of crime.

"It is incumbent on every generation to pay its own debt as it goes. A principle which if acted upon would save one-half the wars of the world"

- Thomas Jefferson

In the Beginning

Let me begin by reiterating for the thousandth time that I was always looking for any opportunity to earn extra money. So prior to attending the police academy, I picked up some side pay by assisting the Jones County Sheriff's Department with some undercover work. Now, my dad had been an officer for the Abilene Police Department, and as a child I bore witness to some of his work; but as for myself, these little jobs with the JCSO were my first real introduction to the field of law enforcement. Then I began receiving the occasional call from the Texas Rangers. They contracted me to assist them with tracking prisoners out in the shinnery. No one knew that country like I did. I enjoyed the work that I did for these two groups, and being freshly laid off from General Dynamics with no prospects for employment, I went in pursuit of a career in law enforcement. I enrolled in and completed the police academy.

During my years as a police officer I also often took weekend jobs providing security at local bars. Two of them in particular contracted me quite often.

One was called Emerald City, and the other bar was known as La Barrio; both were known as places where the drinks were poured and blood was spilled. One weekend, around 1 a.m. a fight broke out at Emerald City and the whole club got involved. Dozens of patrons, drunk on their ass, were fisting each other, throwing glasses and chairs. Hell, even the women were involved. I've never seen so much hair pulling and bitch slapping in all my life. I managed to escape the brawl by crawling out on my hands and knees.

Upon reaching my patrol car, I retrieved a pepper spray grenade and called for back-up. The Abilene Police Department promptly responded by dispatching no less than 20 officers. We finally got the situation under control, cuffing and arresting the offenders. I later inquired as to why APD had responded with so many units. They said when they heard it was me calling for assistance; they knew it must have been a serious situation.

During my time as a police officer, I witnessed one of my academy partners get caught in a "suicide by cop" situation, fatally shooting his suspect. I was attacked when responding to a family disturbance call by the woman I was trying to protect. I watched a baby girl take her last breathe while I held her in my arms … and the list goes on. Fortunately for me, I had the opportunity to change positions early in my career. I was called in and appointed as a member of a task force, where I was later promoted to Task Force Commander. Everything prior to that would prove to be child's play.

Firefight

"I predict future happiness for Americans if they can prevent the government from wasting the labors of the people under the pretense of taking care of them."

— *Thomas Jefferson*

The first firefight I was ever in occurred shortly after I had first become a member of the task force. The Mexican Federales had been clearing a path into the U.S. to get their dope across the border. My team and I had driven south to Presidio, Texas, a border town along the Rio Grande. Presidio would serve as our base during all of our missions. Once we got there, we headed west to a blip on the border called, (ironically), Ruidoso, Texas. Ruidoso is where the pavement stops. There are no cell phone towers, no phone lines, nothing but dirt.

We drove as far in as we could, then hiked through the rocks and hills to where the major crossings were. The lead on our team was showing us green horns where everything was taking place.

We took our positions, hiding in the rocks and waited. Before long we heard the sound of vehicles approaching. It was the Federales. They came screaming into view, loud and boisterous, driving little green trucks, and like a scene out of the Wild West, they came in with guns blazing.

If you've never heard the sound of an AK47, I can tell you it has a distinct ratchet action sound that you will never forget. They were shooting up into the rocks where we were hidden to see if anyone was there.

Time passes slowly when you're scared. We stayed hid and kept quiet for what seemed like two hours, the sound of the Federales raucous bullshit echoing off the rocks, when it became clear others were approaching. It was the mules, the drug runners, in their stolen vehicles, all with Texas tags. The last truck pulled up and we watched one of the runners get paid off, then divvy up the money to all the Federales.

After they got their payoff, the Federales left. As soon as the mules and runners crossed into Texas, we surrounded and arrested them, seized the dope and held it for evidence to be used in the trial. The vehicles were also seized. It was a scenario I would experience time and time again during my run with the task force.

But success, often, is only a veiled mirage. Sometimes you have to pull down the curtain to see what lies behind the façade. The reality is this. After being arrested, the mules and runners would be deported. And the next month they'd be out doing it all again. I can't tell you how many times we took down the same guys, over and over again. The war on drugs is a joke. We'll never stop this corruption as it reaches all the way to the top of our own government.

A lot of us on the task force had families. We made the decision to sign on believing that we were serving our country. We were willing to put our lives on the line and join the fight believing that we could make a difference in the war on drugs. But after a while, if you use your own mind, you start to see that something is just not right.

Pablo Escobar's Son

Yet another trip landed me and my seven man crew down south. We were there to work the southbound traffic in Presidio and patrol the southern border from Alpine to Ruidoso, Texas. If you've never been to Presidio, well you're not missing much, and in the summer months it's hot enough to cook your breakfast on top of your tool box. At any rate, while out patrolling, we decided to drive into Lajitas to have some lunch and meet the Mayor, Clay Henry. There is a restaurant owned by a local Spanish family that has made Lajitas famous for their fajitas, but the real star of this little desert town is their mayor. Mayor Clay Henry is a billy goat, and at that time, there hadn't been a man he'd come up against that could outdrink him.

We all got a good chuckle out of watching that old billy goat drink his beer and went on over to the restaurant to eat. Not long after being seated, a man walked in with two huge bodyguards. Each had Mac 10's under their arms. As always, my crew and I were also armed and now we were on high alert.

The man was Spanish, clean cut and well dressed, and before taking a seat he assessed the room. Spotting us, armed and in our BDU's, he whispered something to his bodyguards and casually walked to our table. The guards, like obedient dogs, stayed where they were. Once at our table he asked who was in charge and I told him I was. Then he asked me if I knew who he was. Indeed I did. His picture has been circulated through most law enforcement and DEA agencies across the county. His name was Juan Pablo Escobar, aka Sebastian Marroquin – son of notorious drug lord, Pablo Escobar.

He assured us that he wanted no trouble and that he just wanted to have lunch. We told him that we, too, were just there to enjoy some fajitas in Lajitas, and were not looking for him. He nodded his head, turned, and motioned for his guards to join him at his table.

I'll have to admit, that was the hardest meal I've ever tried to choke down. His guard dogs were ugly as sin, stood every bit of 6'7", were easily pushing 300 pounds, and they never took their eyes off of us. Finished with their meal, Escobar stood up from his table, and as he walked toward the door, he turned to us, nodded, and said, "You boys be careful." Out the door he went.

Juan Pablo had a price tag on his head. Wanting to distance himself from the violent legacy his father created, he changed his name to Sebastian Marroquin, graduated from college with a degree in architecture and lives a productive life with his wife and daughter. He prefers not to be linked with anything that has to do with his late father.

CHAPTER 2

The Secret, Secret Task Force

"The tree of liberty must be refreshed from time to time with the blood of patriots and tyrants."

– Thomas Jefferson

The U.S. had declared a war on drugs and rather than signing up with the military to fight in some foreign war that I couldn't understand, I thought I could make a difference by staying and fighting the war against drugs. When I agreed to join this secret task force, I, along with six other guys selected from all over the State of Texas who also had the skills, mindset, and physical attributes necessary, were put through a 6 week intense training regime. We were trained by Delta Force, Army Rangers, and one bad ass Israeli commando, all who possessed highly specialized skills.

This was a very challenging training program and was designed to prepare us for field operational environments. Much of our training was conducted in the field and required us to participate in live-fire, field firing activities conducted both day and night, using live ammunition and a wide range of weapons. It was during this training that you discovered exactly what you were made of. During the live fire exercises I watched the biggest, strongest men fall apart under pressure, and, in turn, I've seen the smallest, most unassuming man in the group be the biggest force to be reckoned with. That was the guy you wanted to have your back in a combat situation.

What You Don't Know, Will Hurt You

On one of my missions with the secret task force, we flew into a place in Mexico that was a cocaine lab. This particular lab did it all – manufactured, cut and bagged massive quantities of cocaine.

When we would fly in on these raids, we'd fly in just above the tree tops, to avoid radar detection. If our target location had high points, we'd drop off Angel 1, our sniper, to provide oversight. As we got closer to the lab, we would inevitably start taking small arms fire from the Mexican guards surrounding the lab. Our helicopters had mini-guns mounted on the rails. A mini gun is a modern day version of the Gatling gun and when fired, makes a very unique sound. It is capable of firing thousands of rounds a minute.

The helicopter pilots would bank over these places, and if we were taking fire, we would return fire. We'd come in about two feet off the ground and bail out like mad men while bullets were ricocheting all around. We'd get as far away from the chopper as quickly as possible because when you run missions like that, the chopper becomes a bullet magnet. We called them flying coffins.

When we would raid these drug labs, the workers were typically young Mexican women who we always found naked. In an effort to prevent them from stealing, they were not allowed to wear clothes. At the end of their work shift, every orifice on the women was thoroughly searched. They were slaves, pure and simple.

Once the outside perimeter was secure, we'd go in and

evacuate the building. Then Clint, our demolition man would set the C4 with timers and we would haul ass to our extraction point, which was sometimes miles away. We would signal the chopper for extraction and wait for pick up. Every now and then, bad weather or something else would prevent the chopper from getting to us, and we were left with no choice but to start walking out or hunker down and wait it out. Spending nights in the jungle with Mexican bandits hunting you down made for long, sleepless nights spent on high alert. There were times we would spend two or three days out there waiting to get picked up. We had communications with command, but for whatever reason they couldn't come in. I'm sure it was because they didn't want anyone else to know what we were doing or that we were even there. Bottom line is, it was all kept under the table.

On these missions, we weren't allowed to have any identification. All of our patches, insignias, driver's licenses, or anything that could identify us was strictly forbidden. Keep in mind that this was a secret task force and we all knew if you got caught, as far as the United States was concerned, you didn't exist. We were expendable assets. No one was coming for you. No one you knew, including family, was allowed to know that the task force existed or that you were on it. When you were on a mission, they didn't know where you were. If something happened to you, your family would never know what it was. You were just gone. Those were the facts, and in a roundabout way, you were brainwashed into believing that you were doing all this for your country.

Man Down

Ironically, it was a direct mission on my home turf with the not so secret part of the task force that nearly cost me my life.

Jones County was experiencing an unusual abundance of animal deaths by poachers and our task force was called in to help. Running undercover, we posed as your average weekend hunters. On the appointed night we met up with our suspect and target. We befriended him like fellow good 'ol boys, and took off with him scouring the countryside for game.

It wasn't long afterwards that we spotted a deer off in the distance and the hunt was on. We stopped the truck and our suspect thrust his shotgun out of the passenger side window of the truck, firing several rounds, killing the deer. He laid his 12 gauge shotgun across the seat of the truck. No one could have predicted what happened next.

I got out of the truck and was reaching for my badge when the son of a bitch pulled the trigger – but it wasn't a deer he was aiming at. It was me. The force of the impact lifted me off my feet and blew my 200 pound body across the field. And something else happened in that moment that would change my life forever. As the shot expelled from the barrel of his gun, like a record player slowing down, time stood still. I could actually see the bullet coming at me and felt a hand, or force, literally push me out of the way. And at that instant, the record player sped back up to normal time.

Even stranger is that I wasn't the only one who experienced this slow motion effect. My partner, and the others, experienced it, too, and were totally taken aback. They could only respond with, "Whoa, what just happened here?"

Most people go through life walking only by faith, not by sight - *"Blessed is he who believes and has not seen."* I am one of the fortunate few who have seen with my own eyes that there is a Higher Power who is guiding us through this world, keeping us on our predestined journey.

Instead of suffering a fatal shot that day, I spent the next several months lying flat on my belly healing from the bullet that entered the rear side of one hip, blowing out through the other, narrowly missing my spinal cord. I was told that it was possible that I would never walk again, but that was not in God's plan. Throughout the healing process I never once needed or took any pain medication, and since that day I have lived without fear, for I know, without a doubt, that there is a Higher Power looking after us all.

End of the Road

Over time, the years I spent in the task force began taking a toll on my home life. Conversations about my daily events were not exactly the things you wanted to discuss over pot roast and potatoes with your wife and kids. And so much of my job could not be spoken of - period. The task force required extensive travel, taking me away from home, sometimes for weeks. To make matters worse, I was usually unable to discuss or provide any details of my whereabouts.

Tensions were on the rise and I was in need of an outlet, so I turned to my creative side. I found myself spending most of my evenings alone when I was home, in my shop, where I began making knives, lamps, antler art and leather goods. It was a welcome diversion from the stresses of my day and helped me clear my cluttered mind. As time went on, more often than not, I'd catch myself absorbed in visions of living in a log cabin, nestled amongst the tall pines. The calling to be in the mountains was getting stronger and my dreams were so vivid, yet in reality it all still seemed so far away, so unattainable.

I put my feelers out with Paige about the prospect of moving to the mountains. She made it very clear that she would never entertain the idea of moving, and we continued to grow further and further apart. Eventually, our paths turned in completely opposite directions.

After 24 years of marriage, I filed for divorce. It was the last thing I wanted, and is probably the hardest decision I have ever had to make. But the image in my mind of lying on my death bed wondering, "What if" haunted me. At 38 years old, the voice in my head was my grandfather's: "Don't be like me, son. Go chase your dreams".

Sink or swim, I had to try.

Part Four
In Pursuit of the Dream

CHAPTER **1**

Within Sight

"Society speaks and all men listen; mountains speak and wise men listen."

-John Muir

The divorce was hard on everyone but I'd set my sights on living the life I'd dreamed of since I was child. I was determined to open a trading post where I could sell the Native American art I'd been creating and where I could sell my skins and hides. I was also determined to build the log cabin that I'd drawn as a young boy and live my life in the wilderness where I felt most at peace. I had friends who lived in Ruidoso that I'd visited in the past and I set my sights on the rugged Sierra Blanca mountain range in Lincoln County, New Mexico. I felt a kinship with the land each time I visited and sensed an almost supernatural draw to the area. But first I had to come up with the means to get there.

When my divorce became final, I put my house up for sale, the house I'd built with my own two hands when I was still in my teens. It seemed most everything I'd created in my youth would now provide the means that would carry me to my dream. Everything would have to be sold to make way for the new life I hoped to create.

My Other Half

My house had been on the market for quite some time and, to my disappointment, there had been little interest. I had a little cash left after the divorce but not what it would take to get moved and get my store up and running. I felt like I'd been waiting my entire life and now the next step to pursuing my dream hinged on the sale of my home. I couldn't figure out why it was taking so long. I knew in my heart that the White Mountains were exactly where I was supposed to be. But unbenounced to me, God held one more card that hadn't yet been played. It was the queen of hearts and her name was Barbra.

It was in late October, 2002 that I found myself sitting alone having lunch at a local Taco Bueno when I saw a familiar face walk in the door. I recognized her, but I just couldn't put my finger on from where. When we made eye contact, it was obvious she knew me, too. She smiled and waved, and came over to the table to say hello. It turned out she was the manager of a local employment service I had used while working a part time job at Texas Industrial. Texas industrial was a small fabrication shop I worked at for a short time while working nights as a police officer. She'd made several visits to my office when I was in need of additional employees. We reintroduced ourselves and I asked her to join me. What would have been a quick lunch turned into several hours of talking and laughing. She, too, had just divorced, and as it turned out, both of our divorces were final just two days apart.

We exchanged phone numbers and went our separate ways that day, but I was going to make sure that I saw her again.

Blonde, blue eyed and beautiful, I could sense that she was equally as beautiful on the inside. Believing that there are no accidents, I was certain there was a reason she'd crossed my path. Being the suave, debonair man that I was, I called her a couple of days later and asked her if she'd like to go deer hunting with me. She called me back two days later, and after explaining that she knew nothing about guns or hunting, to my surprise, she said yes.

We spent a lot of time together over the next few months, talking about our plans for the future, our goals and everything in between. I told her about my dreams of living in the mountains, building a log cabin, and running a trading post. She asked me what I was waiting for. Although we'd only known each other a few short months, I knew she was just what I needed and I wanted her with me. I also knew that I didn't have a lot to offer at that time. I was hesitant, but somehow I mustered up the courage to ask her if she thought she would be willing to take a chance on me and move to the mountains of New Mexico. I promised her that if she would be patient and have faith in me that I would see to it that one day she would have everything she ever wanted. She took some time to think about it. To my delight – and surprise - she said yes.

Location, Location, Location

It was late January in 2003 when I received a call from one of my Ruidoso friends. He called to tell me that a prime building in the midtown shopping district had recently been vacated. Since the house still hadn't sold, I was torn about what to do. Barbra and I talked about it and made the decision to take a giant leap of faith. We'd just have to work to make the move, regardless of whether or not the house sold. We packed a few bags and made a quick trip to check out the building. We couldn't have been more excited when we saw that the building was a rustic looking old log cabin with its own parking lot, a rare commodity in midtown Ruidoso. It was perfect for a mountain man trading post. Even better, the building was built in the late 1940's on the Apache reservation and had served as a schoolhouse. In 1962, it was disassembled, moved, and rebuilt in its current location, log by log.

As luck, or the good Lord, would have it, the owner of the building just happened to be in town that weekend and said he'd be happy to meet with us. We met at the shop and the owner asked me what type of business I was hoping to put in his building. I told him about the trading post and he seemed to like my idea. He then asked me if I was a Christian. I assured him that I was. He stuck out his hand and said if I would agree to pay the $1200 per month rent then we had a deal. On a hand shake, the location of my trading post was secured. In the 12 ½ years that we've been in our location, I can count on one hand how many times I've seen him.

We spent the rest of the weekend driving around the village looking for a place to live. It seemed so surreal that I was actually fixing to move to the mountains. My dream was within reach. We put a deposit down on a cute, rustic styled house that was for rent. The house had been somewhat neglected and was in need of some paint and repairs, so I made a deal with the landlord to offset my rent by taking care of the maintenance issues. It was a perfect arrangement considering my house in Hawley still hadn't sold and we still weren't sure how the finances were going to come together to make the move.

Selling the Past

Upon our return to Hawley, we started putting pl.
Barbara and I quit our jobs and I began looking around my
house sizing up what I had that I could sell. It was overwhelm-
ing. I had accumulated 24 years' worth of "stuff" and wasn't
sure where to begin. So, I decided to do what every other
red-blooded American does when faced with the daunting
prospect of moving – I had a garage sale. It was a beautiful,
sunny weekend and the turnout was unbelievable. I sold my
scuba gear, fishing gear, car and motorcycle parts, tools, and
more. I put everything I owned on the market including the
cars I'd built. I sold everything.

During the garage sale, an old man came by and asked me
about a weed whacker I was selling. While we were talking,
he inquired about my house. I said I was selling it and asked
if he was interested. All he said was, "Maybe." I showed him
around and he asked how long I'd owned it. I told him I'd
built it myself 20 years earlier when I was just 18 years old.
"Well," he said. "You must have built it right." Jokingly I told
him if he bought the weed eater that I'd throw in the house.
He thought that was funny. Since he was such a sweet, old
guy I just gave him the weed eater and we said goodbye.

The next morning the phone rang. When I answered, a woman on the other end asked if I had shown my house to a Mr.
Smith. I told her I had. She said, "Well, he's here with the
cash." To which I responded, "You're shitting me." She wasn't.

I took this as yet another sign that I was making the right decision; the pieces were falling into place. After paying off loans

and credit card bills – some I didn't even know I had – there wasn't much left. I pulled out of town with $10,000 cash, my old black pick-up truck, one motorcycle, some tools, and a beautiful woman who was willing to give up the life she knew to take a gamble on a guy in pursuit of a dream.

I thought it would be harder to leave than it was. Hell, I'd lived purt near my whole life next door to my dad in Hawley, Texas. And most everyone made it clear they expected me to fail and return with my tail between my legs. Even so, we said our final goodbyes, and a week later Barbara and I became residents and business owners in the Village of Ruidoso.

A Dream Comes to Life

On May 17, 2003 when the doors to TwoBears ... opened for the first time, I swelled with pride. There I was, 28 years after I'd set foot in that trading post in Colorado as a young boy – the owner of my very own mountain man store. I can still remember the very first item that sold – it was a rustic, barn wood framed picture of Augustus McRae and Captain Call from my all-time favorite movie Lonesome Dove. We've sold a lot of those framed pictures over the years, but at that time, we had very little inventory and even less money to purchase more. For the first few years it was not uncommon to find us still at the store at midnight creating merchandise with our own two hands, and we spent many a night sleeping curled up in a buffalo skin on the cold, wood floor.

We did whatever we could to make extra money during those first few years. Aside from building everything that we sold in the store, I took on side jobs raking pine needles and guiding hunters – and Barbra cleaned houses. We were determined to make it. I had received very little support or encouragement from the folks back home when I left, so I was determined. Failure was not an option.

One day, less than a month after opening our doors, an elderly Apache man from the nearby Mescalero reservation came in to the shop. He walked with the aid of a cane, and he was wearing a large medallion around his neck. I didn't know for sure but I guessed he was a medicine man for the tribe. He didn't speak but spent a long time slowly browsing through the store as if we were under some kind of inspection. He was making Barbra nervous and she quietly asked me what he was doing. I told her to wait and I would explain when he left. As he took his leave, he slowly walked out the door, then stopped and turned to me, giving me a low, left to right wave across his chest. I recognized it as a Native American symbol of acceptance and, as there is no word for goodbye in the native language, it is also commonly known as "till next time." We'd been given his blessing.

Since receiving his blessing that day, the Apache people have shopped with and supported us, buying materials they need for ceremonial regalia, cradleboards, moccasins and other sacred Apache items that are handmade. One wall in our shop is dedicated to items specifically for them. It is their patronage that has carried us through many a lean winter when visitors were few. I have always found it ironic how our building, which was originally a schoolhouse located on the reservation, is now a store in which the Apaches trade and I am honored that I was found worthy of their blessing.

Seeing the Light

Today, as you walk through the doors of my trading post, it is like stepping back into the 1800's. Every inch of the old log walls are covered with rustic, handcrafted Native American and western art, taxidermy mounts, gun and knives. Elk, buffalo, bear and wolf skins are draped from the rafters and antler chandeliers hang from the ceiling. Everywhere you look, you are transported to a simpler time when nature provided our means, our food and our clothing. It is representative of the life I live and who I have always been. It is the dream of a 10 year old boy come to life.

One thing I've learned since opening the trading post is that, like the visit of the medicine man, you never know who will walk through those doors. Willie Nelson has an elk antler guitar stand that I made, as well as one of my custom knives. George Strait has shopped with me, along with several professional athletes and a few other celebrities, many of whom have become some of my dearest friends. But it would be a complete stranger named Dori Evans who walked into the trading post one summer day who would ultimately alter my understanding of myself , and the things I see, in a profound and dramatic way. A mystery was about to unfold.

I have always seen things that, for most of my life, I thought others saw as well. My Cherokee grandmother had the gift of visions and all of my young life we had a strong personal connection. She is the one who named me Two Bears and she was very protective of me. Her life ended just as I entered the age of responsibility and understanding as a young man. We never discussed her gift but, had she lived, I believe we would have. I believe she was waiting for me to come of age. At the time of her passing, she apologized to me but never said for what. Her apology has haunted me throughout my adult life as I didn't understand.

Without going into too much detail, I will tell you that from the time I was a small child I could see colors of light around people, including myself, when I looked in the mirror. Occasionally, I could see things before they actually happened, or as they happened from miles away. As a kid, I thought that everybody experienced the same thing, so I never questioned it. But the older I got, the edgier it made me. Over the years it has become increasingly more prevalent. I pick up on the energy of everything around me and at times it is like an all-out assault on my senses. I see sickness in folks in the form of certain colors. I see turmoil, negativity, good and evil and it invades my very being like a plague.

One summer day while working at the store, a tall blonde woman, who I had never seen before, entered the front door and walked straight up to the counter. She stood quietly for a moment and looked at me intently. Her piercing eyes seemed to be looking through me rather than at me. Finally she spoke, and after we got through the casual greetings, she said matter of factly, "You can see me." "Umm, okaayyyy," I said. "Sure, I can see you." Being persistent and with some urgency, she said, "No, you can *see* me. I look like you, don't I?" It took me a minute to gather myself, but as I really allowed myself to see her, I realized that she did look like me. She had the same energy going on around her that I see on myself when I look in the mirror. She continued the conversation by asking if I knew a Native American woman with long silky hair, and creamy smooth skin. She went on to describe my grand-mother to a tee. She asked if I knew who this woman was and I stammered, "It's my grandmother."

I stood there speechless while Dori explained that she had been sent to me by my grandmother to help me come into, and understand the gift she had passed on to me. My grand-mother had spoken to her in a dream and told her that she was sorry that she had passed on before being able to finish my teaching. Finding a willing subject in Dori , who possessed the gift as well, she sent her in her stead. I invited Dori into the back office where we sat and talked for several hours. She knew things about me that were impossible for her to know.

Since that day, Dori and I have become very close as we share a unique gift that many people do not understand. By raising my understanding of the gift, she has taught me valuable les-sons on how to cope when it begins to overpower my day to day life. I have always trusted my sixth sense. It has served me well and saved my ass many times throughout the years, but now I have learned to rely on it in all aspects of my life.

CHAPTER **2**

Dream Part Deux

Although opening the trading post was the fulfillment of a huge part of my dream, there was another portion yet to be realized. I still carried the sketch I had drawn as a young boy of a log cabin in the woods - and making it a reality was always at the forefront of my mind.

We were meeting lots of new people and making new friends. One friend I met early on invited me to go hunting with him. On the morning of the hunt, we loaded up and he took me all over these mountains. We were driving down a forest service road in Nogal Canyon when we came upon a realtor putting a "For Sale" sign out in front of a piece of property. We pulled over and I visited with him for a bit. The realtor was a long time resident of the area and seemed very knowledgeable about the market. There was something about the property that I was immediately drawn to and I couldn't wait to get home and tell Barbara about it. I felt like a baseball player who had just rounded third base and was heading in for the homerun. There was no question in my mind - I'd found the spot I was going to build my cabin in the woods.

The land was a 2 acre parcel of forest land nestled in between the high ridges of Nogal Canyon. Sitting at 8000' elevation and surrounded by national forest, it was covered in tall pines and black walnut trees. Nogal creek ran from the south end of the property to the north. The land was flat and had the perfect spot to build the cabin of my dreams. Again, we were blessed – this time with a banker who was willing to give us a chance and loan us the money we needed to purchase the land – even though the store was still in its infancy.

We decided that it wasn't feasible for us to continue renting the house in town since the property was located 23 miles north of Ruidoso. We wanted to be on the property while we were building, so we hunted around and picked up a 1982 Hitchhiker 5th wheel. We hauled it out to the property and moved in. The RV didn't have any slide outs so it was pretty tight quarters but, once again, we were determined to make it work. We terminated the lease on our rental house, stored all of our possessions in a sea container, and began our year and a half stay in our new home.

Wild and Wooly

We had our first real encounter with a bear after moving out to the property. We arrived home one evening to discover a black bear who had taken an interest in a freezer we had stored under the tongue of the 5th wheel. It was filled with hamburger, steaks, and elk meat and, frozen as it was, he could smell it and was determined it would be his evening meal. He slapped that freezer around like it was a beach ball, huffing and pouncing on it as if the force of him would break it open. I fired a couple of rounds from my pistol which sent him scampering up the mountain behind the property. Needless to say, our freezer was ruined.

The winter that we spent living in the Hitchhiker was one of the worst winters the area had seen in many years. Snow was packed under the tongue of the 5th wheel with drifts that reached the bottom of the windows. One morning when I woke up, I thought Barbra was laying on my hair, and when I asked her to move, I discovered that she wasn't even in bed. It turned out the condensation had built up inside on the trailer walls and had frozen. Sleeping with my head pressed against the wall, my hair had frozen to the wall, too.

All the same, we broke ground on the house in July, 2004 and once we got the log shell of the house dried in, Barbra and I began working on the inside. We'd close up shop in the evening, head home and grab something to eat. Then we'd flip on some lights and heaters and go to work framing doorways and windows, building cabinets, laying tile and painting. In October, 2005, we said goodbye to the Hitchhiker and moved in to the log cabin I'd sketched as a young boy.

CHAPTER **3**

The Wolves

I've always been drawn to wolves. We have a lot in common. Maybe it's because of their instinctiveness and ability to see beyond the physical that I feel a special bond with them. I respect their hunting prowess and ability to move through nature with stealth and focus. And I understand their pack mentality and hierarchy. It's a natural order. There is an alpha who leads and every member of the pack knows their place. They're fiercely protective of their own and will fight to the death to protect what's theirs. I relate to that on a very deep level so it was only natural that, when were able to stake our own claim in the forest, bringing wolves into our pack would be a priority. It was always part of my dream.

In September, 2004, while living in the Hitchhiker, we brought our first wolf child home. Kodi, who is ¾ arctic wolf and ¼ malamute, was just three weeks old when he arrived. He slept on my chest and I bottle fed him until he was old enough to be weaned. Two weeks after we brought him home I traded a buckskin shirt I'd made for his brother Bear.

After the boys got to be a few years old, we brought in Smoki, a female timber wolf. Wolves mate for life and Smoki chose Bear as her mate. They are still together. Not wanting Kodi to be alone, we eventually located and acquired another female, Nikita. Kodi and Nikita never truly bonded, and it was becoming apparent that Kodi was going to be our "lone wolf." Nikita left us and when Smoki and Bear finally produced a black female, we kept her. We named her Kimber and began our search for her mate. That's when we adopted the fifth member of our pack, Cherokee and the two hit it off.

Kodi is allowed to run loose and never wanders far from my side. He is the first to greet visitors and is a devoted companion. He always keeps a watchful eye on me and Barbra. We are connected on a much deeper plane. We are connected in spirit.

People often ask what I feed our wolves. Sometimes I am certain that they eat as good as, if not better than I do! During trapping and hunting seasons, I keep and use everything I harvest - the meat, claws, bones, teeth, fur – all of it. The furs get sent out for tanning, I use the claws in my artwork, and the meat gets chopped up and fed to the pack throughout the year. I try to keep their diet consistent with what they would eat in the wild. That is why my wolves stay strong and healthy.

Though my wolves are hybrids, they have a high percentage of wolf genes and can only be domesticated to a degree. Their wild instincts remain strong. By nature, they are binge eaters. They'll eat and eat and eat, gorging themselves all at one meal, and then not eat for two days. That's how it is when you're hunting in the wild. You get lucky one day and two days you don't.

We've created a wolf sanctuary on our property where our pack has the room they need to run and live. The bond and companionship I have with my five wolf hybrids is the most rewarding relationship I've had out of all my animals. Their haunting howl at 5 a.m. every morning is very humbling and peaceful and lets me know they are happy, like they are singing to me their song of love.

In the Wild

One of my favorite sayings is a Native American proverb that reads:

An old Cherokee man once told his grandson, "My son, there is a battle between two wolves inside us all. One is Evil; it is anger, jealousy, greed, resentment, inferiority, lies, and ego. The other is Good; it is joy, peace, love, hope, humility, kindness, & truth."

The boy thought about it and asked, "Grandfather, which wolf wins?"

The old man quietly replied, "The one you feed."

The wolf story is a double edged tale. Folks need to remember that the wolf was here first. That being said, humans are here now and we must strive to find balance amidst all species.

With the wolves here there is a God given balance to life for all. The wolf eats the elk and bison and keeps nature in balance. With the elk and bison herds managed, grasses can grow tall and the streams deep, fish remain abundant, otters and beaver are plentiful. Then it was decided that man should kill the wolf. This was done so that the sheep and cows that man raised for food could survive; after all, we have to eat as well. At the root of all this was money, more specifically, the loss of it, as ranchers were losing money with the wolves decimating their livestock. No one wants to starve, so we killed the wolves.

Man thought, misguidedly, that there was harmony for them

now that the wolf was gone, but nothing could have been further from the truth.

There was a study done in Yellowstone National Park in regards to the wolves. The study was done over the course of 10 years and here's what they found. Without the balance of Mother Nature and the wolves, the elk and bison multiplied, as well as the sheep and cattle, and man prospered. New businesses sprung up along with outfitters for all the abundant game. Money was flowing! There came to be so many elk and bison in the park that they ate all the grass along the banks of the rivers, allowing the water to wash away the banks, widening the rivers to the point of being too shallow for the fish to swim.

Of course, no fish meant no otter or beavers, no plants, no flowers, no bees or birds - all were gone! Their food source was gone. Mother Nature was not in balance now. So wildlife biologists reintroduced wolves back into the park; they ate well, balanced the elk and bison herds and grass began to grow again along the river banks. With that came the fish and all that fed on them, putting everything back into balance - except man's loss of livestock - and now there was not enough game for the outfitters to hunt meaning a loss of money and jobs.

Herein lies the dilemma - how to balance it all. How do we live together in harmony? It's simple, remove the monetary issues. Right now there are too many people on this planet for there ever to be balance. If we could return to the Native American way of life, we could, like my ancestors, live with all nature and find balance. But in this age of modern man, our nation will have to be set back, or reset, by war or disease and relearn how to live on this earth with respect.

Some will say that wolves are indiscriminate killers. This is not true. Another study was done where there were animals killed by the wolf and not eaten. However, when the blood of the deceased animal was tested, it came back positive for CWD (Chronic Wasting Disease) now found in most elk and deer populations. CWD comes from the pollutants in the rivers and streams. The wolves can taste the bad blood and choose not to eat it. Nothing else eats it either, not even the ravens. The diseased carcass will lay there rotting until the worms and flies consume it.

With all this being said, I ask that before you complain about the wolves being a nuisance remember that you destroyed their habitat to build your own.

CHAPTER **4**

Settling In

SO MANY OF my dreams had come to fruition; I was living in the mountains, running my very own Mountain Man trading post, and had just moved in to my log cabin. Life couldn't have been any better for me – no more drug cartels, no more nights in the jungles of Mexico, no more hidden life. I was free to be me; to build and sell my artwork, to hunt and trap in the mountains, to live life on my terms.

Over the years, I've been told by many locals that if the mountain wants you here, you will prosper... if not, you will not succeed, despite your best efforts. All doors have opened for me since I made the heartfelt decision to pursue my dreams. It was as if God was telling me that I'd paid my dues and that he would shine his light on the path I was to follow.

Living the Life

As a boy I had run a trap line to make extra money to buy school clothes and other necessities. Now that I'd found my-self in the mountains, surrounded by national forest, and an abundance of animals, I decided to start trapping again, like a real mountain man.

Trapping season runs in the winter months. That is when the animals have the best pelts, but it makes trapping a bit more challenging than it was in the shinnery. Heading out into the woods at 5 a.m. on a snowy winter morning can be brutal. It's sometimes bitter cold, with temperatures dropping down into the low teens, and if you can find your traps after a heavy snow, odds are they'll be frozen. All the same, hiking along the trails, breathing in the clean, crisp mountain air, hearing the chatter of the squirrels and the singing birds is still one of my favorite ways to start the day. On those cold winter morn-ings, if I was lucky enough to catch a fox, a coyote, or even a bobcat - well, that was just the icing on the cake. I would tan the pelts and sell them in the store or I would use them in the artwork I created. The meat was always fed to the wolves.

It wasn't always a surreal experience – sometimes it was just down right funny. I took Barbra with me one cold and snowy morning to run my trap line. Despite wearing layers of warm clothing, the poor girl was freezing to death. We got to the fifth trap on my line and I could see that it had been tripped. I headed over to reset it and clean around the area while she grabbed my bag containing all my supplies. Carefully, I reset the trap and asked Barbra to hand me my stink bait. Now, if you're not familiar with stink bait, it is what the name implies.

It is the most foul smelling mix of fermented raw meat, organs, entrails and blood you can concoct. Barbara opened the container and handed it to me, and with her gloved hand, she wiped her cold, runny nose. The next thing I knew, Barbra was turning green and gagging. She'd gotten a little bit of that stink bait on her glove when she opened it and ran it right into her nose. I could not contain my laughter. That was the last time she went out on the trap line with me.

Sometimes the pelts come a little easier. Occasionally, the New Mexico Department of Game and Fish wardens will be called upon to deal with a nuisance bear. A bear that has gotten desensitized to humans can be dangerous, and after having been tagged three times, the animal will be euthanized. Knowing that I make every effort to use any and all parts of an animal so its life is not lost in vain, the game wardens will bring it to me. There have been many a Friday night that plans for an evening out have unexpectedly turned into a night skinning and cleaning a bear.

Alaska, The Last Frontier

There are still times when my thirst for adventure takes me far from home. In 2010, three good friends and I decided we wanted to hunt and fish in Alaska - The Last Frontier. Barbra and I had made the trip a few years earlier but during that trip I was plagued with an 8mm kidney stone. Needless to say, we didn't have much fun. We were excited to have another shot at it.

After all the arrangements were made, we loaded up with enough gear to last us two weeks and headed off to Albuquerque where we caught a flight to Anchorage. We landed at 2:00 a.m., grabbed our luggage and gear, and set out to locate our accommodations for the next two weeks, a rented R.V. Since there wasn't much we could do at 2 a.m. in Anchorage, Alaska, we bunked down for the remainder of the night, but as soon as the sun was up, we were raring to go. All of us were anxious to get the trip started. We loaded up on groceries and fishing gear and headed out on one of the five highways that runs through the great state of Alaska. We'd stop by a river or one of the many lakes, catch some fresh fish for dinner, and we'd spend the night right there on the side of the road. Every day offered an unforgettable memory, whether it was the majestic mountains and glaciers, the powerful bald eagles that seemed to follow us, or the abundance of diverse wildlife that we encountered.

One day we ended up in Valdez and decided to do some gold prospecting. We chose a location known as Gold Gulch, figuring with a name like that the odds would be in our favor. Patience is a virtue when it comes to gold panning, and my patience paid off that day when I found a nugget that weighed in at 6 grams. I couldn't believe my luck. Today it hangs from a gold chain around Barbra's neck.

The very next day we went on a salmon run. I caught the first salmon; it was big enough to feed us all that night … and we sure would've enjoyed it, but when I got the fish close enough to scoop it up in the net, a huge eagle swooped down from out of nowhere and with its great talons, snatched it up and soared majestically off into the horizon with our dinner. We all just stood there looking at each other in disbelief. While the eagle was feasting on my salmon high up in its nest, we were having bologna and pork and beans for dinner. But, as luck would have it, we more than made up for the loss on a Halibut fishing trip we took later that week. I've done a lot of fishing in my life, but I have never seen so many fish come up with fangs. Ugly aside, I sent home 160 pounds of Halibut fillets.

By journey's end we had traversed across the entire state of Alaska, travelling all five highways from as far south as Ketchikan to as far north as the Denali National Park where we spent a few nights soaking in the breathtaking views of Mt. McKinley.

Little Bear

June 4, 2012 was a day that those who live in Lincoln County will never forget. Lightning struck on the back side of Ski Apache in an area that hadn't been logged or deforested - *ever*. The thick, deadfall of timber and pine caught fire and those in charge decided to let it burn, classifying it as a controlled burn. But there was nothing controlled about it.

The fire fed heartily on our dense forest, consuming everything in its path, and the raging inferno was headed our way. We could see the red glow of the fire just over the ridge and knew that if it jumped into our canyon, it would funnel through and there'd be no escaping. When we were evacuated from our home, we were only able to take a few of our personal belongings

For the following three days we would have no idea if we would have a home to return to or whether our animals would survive. I just kept thinking that surely I wasn't brought here, my dreams fulfilled, to have it end like this. To this day I have no idea who made the call to Barbra's cell phone to inform us that they were planning to do a back-burn on the ridge right behind our house, saying they would clear us to get through the road blocks if we wanted to get our animals. That was the first news we'd received in three days. Hearing that we still *had* a home, and that our animals were still alive was indeed good news. We jumped in the truck and were heading for home when we ran into a road block. The officer who was manning the block had black and white orders that no one was to get through without an escort. When it became apparent that he was not going to cooperate, I told him who I was and asked him to radio in a special code that would allow him to obtain information about me - who I was and what security clearances I had. The officer gave me a puzzled look but did as I requested. He returned with a fresh, friendlier attitude and cleared us to go on through - unescorted. Barbra and the friends following us were dumbfounded. My past had once again served me well.

The security officer opened the blockade allowing us to pass through and we began the long, eerie drive to our home. It was surreal as we drove through the thick layer of smoke. There were several hot spots still smoldering and many of the homes I passed by every day had been reduced to nothing more than a pile of smoldering ash. The trees that give these mountains so much life were now torched - and there was nothing moving. It looked like a war zone at the end of a lengthy battle.

When we finally arrived home to evacuate for the second time, I was thankful that my cabin and my animals had survived. We walked the property and found many burn scars where flying embers had landed all around the place, even on our deck – but the home that we'd built with our blood, sweat, and tears did not burn. The Great Spirit had blessed us once again.

A hot shot crew from Idaho was stationed and working in our canyon. These guys functioned like a well-oiled machine. They were impressive. We met the supervisor who was assigned to our canyon; he advised us that plans had changed and they would not be conducting a back burn behind our home. He told us that, in his opinion, we were safe to stay. So, when the five sheriff's deputies arrived in an attempt to force us to evacuate, I refused to go. We agreed that if the hot shot crews were to leave the canyon due to threatening conditions, we would follow. We told the deputies that although there was heavy smoke hanging in the air, and a blazing inferno just over the next ridge, we were more comfortable staying at our home. We did not leave again, and instead we provided coffee and lunch for many of the hot shot crews that were working in and around our place. We became "command central."

In the fifteen days the fire burned out of control, it damaged or destroyed over 224 residences, 10 outbuildings, and caused $11.5 million in damages, decimating 38,000 acres of our pristine forest - proving that you truly cannot control a burn. Many say that its Mother Nature's way of rejuvenating the land. It also has been said that it is a 30 year event. I will never understand why standing dead trees are not harvested and sold as timber; it would provide a means to generate revenue for the state and contribute to the maintenance of a healthy forest. But that's just my opinion, and well, nobody asked me.

A Purpose and a Plan

"In the beginning of a change, the patriot is a scarce man, and brave, and hated, and scorned. When his cause succeeds, the timid join him, for then, it costs nothing to be a patriot"

-Mark Twain

The years I worked in the field of law enforcement opened my eyes to the extent of the corruption that runs rampant throughout all levels of our government. Government corruption has become so endemic in our society that most people have just accepted it. The American people should be furious.

I know as well as anyone, most folks feel as though their hands are tied. I've always believed that someday the good people of this country will tire of the bullshit and that we will find ourselves engaged in another civil war – only this time it will be the people vs. the government in an effort to take back our country; however, never once, did I think it would happen during my lifetime.

We are living in a strange time right now, and with my ability to see things, it is clear that many, many people are angry. They're angry that they've lost their jobs and are unable to find work; angry because no matter how hard they work they can barely support their families; angry that the cost of living has skyrocketed and wages haven't; angry that they are being forced to buy unaffordable healthcare – the list goes on.

My sixth sense has been working overtime lately and it tells me that something is about to change. Quite frankly, something needs to change as we cannot continue on like we have been. Not knowing when or what is lurking in the future, the only thing I know to do is to be prepared for anything – and I am. Yes, I store food and supplies and prepare to protect what is mine should anything occur.

I believe that the Great Spirit has brought me to where I am today for a reason. Whether it was to see the fulfillment of my dream or to help others prepare, so be it. Either way, I am grateful. TwoBears Trading post will be celebrating its 13th anniversary in 2016 and a new photo for our anniversary wall will be generated. I can't be sure what the future holds for us but if it was decided that my time on this earth was over today, I will die a happy man for I have pursued and achieved my dreams, have travelled all over this world, and above all, I have walked on this earth without fear knowing that there is a God and he has a plan for everyone, including me.

TwoBears Trading Post "Anniversary Wall"

I'd like to give a special note of thanks to Kelly Brooks, a devoted journalist, editor, and friend, and my wife, Barbra for the countless hours they have contributed to putting this book together. Without them my story would not have made it to publication.

Me and Kodi warming up by the fire

Epilogue: The Wife's Perspective

I wasn't looking for a relationship, - hell, I was just getting out of one- but nobody really ever goes looking for love do they; love has its own way of finding you. Fate had given me a special opportunity that day I stopped at my favorite Taco Bueno to grab some lunch. Walking in I saw one of my customers sitting alone so I waved to acknowledge him and went over to say hello. He invited me to join him and I did. He was the fabrication supervisor for a company that occasionally called on me to provide temporary workers. I had made several sales and service calls to his office but until this day, our conversations had always been business related and strictly professional. Obviously the veil that I shrouded myself with when working prevented me from noticing his piercing blue eyes that were now looking into my very soul.

He was very easy to talk to and it turned out that we were both going through a divorce-filed just two days apart! I was enjoying his company so much that time had totally gotten away from me; we'd been sitting there for over 2 hours!!

I'm not sure I've ever truly believed in love at first sight, besides, this wasn't first sight, however, It was my first look Into who he was on a personal level; Intriguing, intelligent, and ambitious. But after we said our goodbyes, I drove away, certain that this was the man I was supposed to spend the rest of my life with. I'd never been so sure of anything in my life.

I couldn't get him off my mind and hoped I would hear from him. When I did, he was calling to ask me out on what would be our first "date"....not dinner, not a movie, but an 11 day deer hunt in New Mexico! Now, the only hunting I had ever done was while looking for my lost golf ball and I definitely didn't know anything about guns, so naturally I was a little apprehensive. After giving it some thought and knowing I would be in good hands, I said yes. Besides, I'm always up for a new adventure!

The trip was fabulous. We were totally away from the stress and distractions that the city brings and were at one with nature. I learned much over those 11 days and was even introduced to some wildlife that I had never heard of, much less seen. Hiking, hunting, and blazing campfires at night proved to be the best first date ever.

The more time we spent together, the more enthralled with this man I became. He had dreams and aspirations, and he was unlike anyone I had ever known. He told me he'd had dreams of living in the mountains, running his own trading post, and building a log cabin since he was just a young boy, but somehow life had just gotten in the way. I couldn't help but think it was more than a coincidence that the mountain town he was considering moving to happened to be the very same one I had, as a child, also dreamed of moving to; Ruidoso, New Mexico. During my childhood and into my teenage years, Ruidoso was where my family spent many winter vacations. We were regulars on the snow packed ski slopes of Sierra Blanca, now known as Ski Apache. I always loved that mountain village.

Mark was the epitomy of tall, dark, and handsome and had ruggedness about him that I loved, but there was also this Intense, dangerous side to him. When he looked at me with those eyes, I felt naked and vulnerable, like I didn't belong to myself anymore-not completely. I knew that I belonged to him, and that he was it for me. Without any doubt, I knew we'd been brought together for a reason and that I would never leave his side. So when he asked if I'd consider moving to Ruidoso with him and start a new life together, after some consideration, I said yes. I couldn't help but question whether or not I was letting my emotions take over and could I be making a mistake.... after all, this was still a new relationship, but as I said earlier, my heart was telling me that this was the man God had sent me; to love and be loved by. So, taking down all my walls of protection, I took a giant leap of faith and decided to go full throttle. Besides, trading in my "Corporate America" job for a life in the mountains, with the man of my dreams, and being our own boss definitely had me excited.

We made the move to New Mexico and worked hard together to realize Marks lifelong dreams of living in the mountains, owning his own mountain man trading post, and living in that log home he had always visualized. Then, in 2010, Mark gave me the greatest gift of all – his name. We were married at the top of Nogal peak, a place that is and always will be special to us.

Mr. & Mrs.

I was, and still am, so amazed by Mark's creativity and the level of skill he possesses. He has a remarkable ability to accomplish anything. Whether its electrical, plumbing, carpentry, building guns or cars, there hasn't been a task or project set before him that he didn't know how to do. I've asked him many times how it is that he knows how to do so many things, his only answer is , "I'm not sure, I just know." He seems to have an infinite source of knowledge to pull from. I've always wondered what it would be like to live in his head if only for one day!

He also has very powerful energy and is somewhat of an enigma. Over the years I have watched people interact with Mark and they are either intimidated by him, or they aspire to be just like him. Hell, even the hummingbirds are drawn to him. It's nothing for me to look outside and see them landing on him as he sits quietly in the gazebo writing in his journal.

It hasn't always been easy since we've moved here to New Mexico but together we have learned that we can accomplish whatever we set our minds to. We have definitely put in our time to get where we are today. The life we have created is very rewarding as we strive to live a self-sufficient lifestyle; hunting, gardening, canning and preserving our own food, and living off our land as much as we can. It is a lifestyle I was meant for. My grandmother, who just recently passed on, introduced me to this way of life at a very early age; I know that she watches over us with pride.

꩜꩜꩜

My "Commander" is many things, but above all, he is a man of honor and a man of his word; a man I am proud to call my husband. My only regret is that I didn't know him sooner but I pray that we have a long journey ahead of us that continues to be filled with love and laughter, and adventure. I do believe there is a time and place for everything. And this is our time.

Barbra and Kodi

Photo Album

My '29 Coupe as it ended up before I sold to get to the mountains.

'23 Ford C-Cab

Old Trappers Cabin I built at the end of our property using logs reclaimed from burned out areas.

Playing aound with my grandsons Evan and Ja'Kobe.

Heading out to run the traps.

My Grandma and Grandpa, in their later years.

Hiking the Tetons

Catching Dinner during my hike across the Tetons.

Cherokee

Fur Trading with Tom Oar and Will Stringfellow

CPSIA information can be obtained
at www.ICGtesting.com
Printed in the USA
FSOW01n1745131216
28536FS